D0071816

*The*

# Dominican
# Americans

**Other Titles in
The New Americans Series**
Ronald H. Bayor, Series Editor

The South Asian Americans
*Karen Isaksen Leonard*

The Cuban Americans
*Miguel Gonzalez-Pando*

The Taiwanese Americans
*Franklin Ng*

The Korean Americans
*Won Moo Hurh*

# The Dominican Americans

*Silvio Torres-Saillant*
*and*
*Ramona Hernández*

**THE NEW AMERICANS**
Ronald H. Bayor, Series Editor

**GREENWOOD PRESS**
**Westport, Connecticut • London**

**Library of Congress Cataloging-in-Publication Data**

Torres-Saillant, Silvio.
    The Dominican Americans / Silvio Torres-Saillant and Ramona
Hernández.
        p.   cm.—(New Americans ; 1092–6364)
    Includes bibliographical references (p.   ) and index.
    ISBN 0–313–29839–4 (alk. paper)
    1. Dominican Americans.   I. Hernández, Ramona.   II. Title.
III.  Series: New Americans (Westport, Conn.)
E184.D6T67   1998
973'.04687293—DC21          97–37491

British Library Cataloguing in Publication Data is available.

Library of Congress Catalog Card Number: 97–37491
ISBN: 0–313–29839–4
ISSN: 1092–6364

First published in 1998

Greenwood Press, 88 Post Road West, Westport, CT 06881
An imprint of Greenwood Publishing Group, Inc.

Printed in the United States of America

The paper used in this book complies with the
Permanent Paper Standard issued by the National
Information Standards Organization (Z39.48–1984).

10 9 8 7 6 5 4 3 2 1

# Contents

# Illustrations

## TABLES AND FIGURES

## PHOTOS

# Series Foreword

Oscar Handlin, a prominent historian, once wrote, "I thought to write a history of the immigrants in America. Then I discovered that the immigrants were American history." The United States has always been a nation of nations where people from every region of the world have come to begin a new life. Other countries such as Canada, Argentina, and Australia also have had substantial immigration, but the United States is still unique in the diversity of nationalities and the great numbers of migrating people who have come to its shores.

Who are these immigrants? Why did they decide to come? How well have they adjusted to this new land? What has been the reaction to them? These are some of the questions the books in this "New Americans" series seek to answer. There have been many studies about earlier waves of immigrants— e.g., the English, Irish, Germans, Jews, Italians, and Poles—but relatively little has been written about the newer groups—those arriving in the last thirty years, since the passage of a new immigration law in 1965. This series is designed to correct that situation and to introduce these groups to the rest of America.

Each book in the series discusses one of these groups, and each is written by an expert on those immigrants. The volumes cover the new migration from primarily Asia, Latin America, and the Caribbean, including: the Koreans, Cambodians, Filipinos, Vietnamese, South Asians such as Indians and Pakistanis, Chinese from both China and Taiwan, Haitians, Jamaicans, Cubans, Dominicans, Mexicans, Puerto Ricans (even though they are already U.S. citizens), and Jews from the former Soviet Union. Although some of these people, such as Jews, have been in America since colonial times, this series concentrates on their recent migrations, and thereby offers its unique contribution.

These volumes are designed for high school and general readers who want to learn more about their new neighbors. Each author has provided information about the land of origin, its history and culture, the reasons for migrating, and the ethnic culture as it began to adjust to American life. Readers will find fascinating details on religion, politics, foods, festivals, gender roles, employment trends, and general community life. They will learn how Vietnamese immigrants differ from Cuban immigrants and, yet, how they are also alike in many ways. Each book is arranged to offer an in-depth look at the particular immigrant group but also to enable readers to compare one group with the other. The volumes also contain brief biographical profiles of notable individuals, tables noting each group's immigration, and a short bibliography of readily available books and articles for further reading. Many contain a glossary of foreign words and phrases.

Students and others who read these volumes will secure a better understanding of the age-old questions of "who is an American" and "how does the assimilation process work?" Similar to their nineteenth-and early twentieth-century forebears, many Americans today doubt the value of immigration and fear the influx of individuals who look and sound different from those who had come earlier. If comparable books had been written one hundred years ago they would have done much to help dispel readers' unwarranted fears of the newcomers. Nobody today would question, for example, the role of those of Irish or Italian ancestry as Americans; yet, this was a serious issue in our history and a source of great conflict. It is time to look at our recent arrivals, to understand their history and culture, their skills, their place in the United States, and their hopes and dreams as Americans.

The United States is a vastly different country than it was at the beginning of the twentieth century. The economy has shifted away from industrial jobs; the civil rights movement has changed minority-majority relations and, along with the women's movement, brought more people into the economic mainstream. Yet one aspect of American life remains strikingly similar—we are still the world's main immigrant receiving nation and as in every period of American history, we are still a nation of immigrants. It is essential that we attempt to learn about and understand this long-term process of migration and assimilation.

Ronald H. Bayor
Georgia Institute of Technology

# *Acknowledgments*

We shall express our gratitude to all concerned by narrating the chain of events that brought this book to fruition. Almost two years ago, Yale University professor Patricia Pessar informed us about Greenwood's ethnic cultural heritage series, the "New Americans" series, which envisioned a volume on Dominicans. As the best-known and most-prolific scholar on Dominican migration to the United States, Professor Pessar had been invited to write it but could not accept due to a commitment at the time with another publisher for a book on the same subject. She recommended us, and we deeply appreciate her generosity and trust.

Professor Pessar no doubt had us in mind at the time because of our connection with the CUNY Dominican Studies Institute at the City College of New York, which had already attained a measure of visibility in the academic community nationwide. We owe gratitude to the Dominican Institute for existing and to those who have contributed to its existence, beginning with Dominican students at the City University of New York.

During the spring of 1989, students throughout the university campuses went on strike and took over buildings to protest the proposed tuition hike that many feared would deny the children of the poor and the working class access to higher education. Dominican students figured among the leaders of the upheaval. Having participated in the "illegal" occupation of public property, many students faced the possibility of expulsion or incarceration. It dawned on some Dominican faculty in the university that, unlike the other students with whom they shared the leadership of the unrest, Dominican students lacked the support and protection of a university-based faculty organization. At that point, several CUNY faculty and staff, along with some public schoolteachers, established the Council of Dominican Educators to advocate on behalf of Dominican students. The initial council leadership included Ana García Reyes, Luis Alvarez-López, Anthony Stevens Acevedo, Franklin Gutiérrez, Ofelia Rodríguez, Fausto de la Rosa, Nelson Reynoso, and the authors of this book. Subsequently, they would be joined by Belkys Navas, Josefina Báez, Nancy López, and Belkys Necos. They deserve credit for defending Dominican students at a crucial time and for conceiving the idea of proposing to CUNY a university-based Dominican studies unit.

When a new chancellor of the City University of New York came on board in the fall of 1990, the Council of Dominican Educators met with her, and she embraced the idea of a Dominican research venture in CUNY. The council's credibility before Chancellor W. Ann Reynolds was indubitably enhanced by the alliance we had made with the Puerto Rican Council on Higher Education, then led by Edgar Rodríguez, and the CUNY African American Network, headed at that time by Donald Smith. We thank our black and Puerto Rican colleagues for their timely support, and we are indebted to Chancellor Reynolds for her initial approval of the Dominican research initiative. All the steps we subsequently took toward the creation of the CUNY Dominican Studies Institute hinged on her initial assent.

The Dominican Institute drew largely on the model of the Centro de Estudios Puertorriqueños at Hunter College, CUNY. The selfless solidarity of the old guard of the Centro's staff, chiefly Frank Bonilla, Camille Rodríguez, Antonio Lauria, Rina Benmayor, and Iraida López, made all the difference. The insight and caring of Centro associate and former CUNY trustee María Josefa Canino did much for the health of the Dominican Institute.

Former CUNY trustee Gladys Carrión was instrumental in garnering support for the Dominican Institute at the central administration of City University. Similarly, Hostos Community College president Isaura Santiago Santiago and Augusta Souza Kappner, who served as City College acting president in academic year 1992–1993, demonstrated their faith that the time was right for the Dominican Institute to come into being and to thrive as a leader of Dominican studies in the nation.

We are particularly appreciative for the expert technical assistance of the Dominican Institute's administrative coordinator, Sarah Aponte, a library science specialist who has vast knowledge of the bibliography on Dominicans in the United States. Her recommendation of seldom-cited writings that deserved consideration proved invaluable in the preparation of our book. Ms. Aponte generously shared with us the manuscript of her own forthcoming publication, *Dominican Migration in the United States: An Annotated Bibliography*, which we used to advantage on several occasions.

Finally, we are indebted to those who took time to read our drafts. Historian Frank Moya Pons perused the text of chapter 1 and made suggestions that improved our account of U.S.-Dominican relations. Fiction writer Junot Díaz read most of the manuscript with great enthusiasm. His critical input especially in chapter 4 brought to our attention key stylistic nuances that we did not hesitate to address. Finally, educator Anthony Stevens-Acevedo helped in reading the galleys. Of course, the authors remain sole proprietors of any defects in the form or content of this book.

# *Preface*

People from the Dominican Republic have massively moved out of their home country in search of a better life in North America. Although there has been a Dominican presence in the United States at least since the late nineteenth century, the great exodus of Dominicans from their native land and the development of Dominican immigrant settlements here date from the mid-1960s. The size of this community in the United States grew tremendously in the 1970s and 1980s. According to the U.S. census, in 1990 511,297 Dominicans were living as permanent residents in the United States; over 65% of them were residing in the state of New York. But the actual size of the community is much larger because the official figures do not account for undocumented residents, whose number is presumed high. The influx of Dominicans, who outnumbered all other immigrants coming into New York City and ranked number six in the entire nation, continued growing into the 1990s. New York City received an average of 22,028 Dominican immigrants per year between 1990 and 1994 (Lobo and Salvo 1997: 16).

The rest of the Dominican population in the United States is spread throughout the country, with the most numerous contingents residing—in descending order—in the following states: New Jersey, Florida, Massachusetts, Rhode Island, Connecticut, California, Maryland, Texas, Pennsylvania, and Washington. An examination of the socioeconomic conditions of Dominicans in each of the states and cities where they have come to live over the last three decades would require a more specialized study than the length of this book would allow. We, therefore, will concentrate on the state of New York, particularly the five counties of the city of New York, as the most appropriate setting to illustrate the weaknesses and strengths, the challenges and possibilities of Dominican immigrants in the receiving society. New York is a center of Dominican life in the United States, not the only one, of course, but we believe it can represent the community nationally. We hold the view that how Dominicans fare in New York will largely decide their fate as an ethnic minority in the rest of the United States.

*The Dominican Americans* deals with the experience of a settled community in its North American abode. The book begins with a brief historical background that traces the geographical, cultural, and ethnic origins of the Dominican people. Chapter 1 gives an account of U.S.-Dominican relations, beginning in the mid-1800s, in which the United States often took the initiative, including a period of eight years when the Dominican Republic had an American government. Chapter 2 surveys the political and socioeconomic conditions that have caused Dominicans to leave their home country en masse since the mid-1960s. The rise of a Dominican community in the United States is the subject of chapter 3, which surmises the insertion of these immigrants into the labor market, education, business, politics, and the professions, and assesses the barriers and possibilities they face. Chapter 4 maps the development of a Dominican culture that stems from the immigrant experience, stressing the areas of visual and performing arts, literature, popular music, food, and religion, as well as changed notions of gender and race. Finally, chapter 5 articulates a vision of the future for the Dominican community in the United States.

This book provides a general introduction to Dominicans as a people in the United States, closing a serious gap in the bibliography on American ethnic groups. The authors are part of a small but already significant cohort of academics working in American universities who are contributing to disseminating information about the Dominican experience. Born in the Dominican Republic, we both came to this country in 1973 and received our post-secondary education here. We claim a privileged vantage point. As scholars, we bring to the study of the Dominican community a sound familiarity with the invaluable body of knowledge bequeathed by non-Dominican observers of the community. But also, as members of the group under study, we enjoy access to a view from within. We would like to think that this book draws on a healthy combination of scholarly rigor and social intimacy with our subject. Finally, we should address the demand of Silvia Torres, a teacher at Francis Scott Key Junior High School in Brooklyn, who challenged the propriety of our using the term Dominican Americans to describe the people under perusal. In Latin America and the Hispanophone Caribbean, the word America refers to the Western Hemisphere as a whole. When in 1507 the

German cartographer Martin Waldseemüller proposed to name "the new world" America, in honor of Amerigo Vespucci, he had in mind specifically the Caribbean and South America, the only lands that had up to then been viewed by Europeans. Dominicans come from a region called America. To call them Dominican Americans, then, is repetitious. We admit that the term is problematic, but we shall not reject its use for now, if anything, because negotiating nomenclature is also part of the predicament of the immigrant.

# Introduction: A Brief Historical Background

## THE LAND

Dominicans come originally from the Dominican Republic, a country that occupies the eastern two-thirds of the island of Hispaniola, or, in Spanish, Española, which is located between Cuba and Puerto Rico. The Republic of Haiti occupies the remaining western third of the island. Hispaniola is the second largest of the Greater Antilles in the Caribbean archipelago. Situated about 600 miles southeast of Florida and 310 miles north of Colombia and Venezuela, the Dominican Republic is flanked on the north by the Atlantic Ocean and on the south by the Caribbean Sea. The country's landscape is marked topographically by its three main *cordilleras* (mountain ranges): the Oriental, the Septentrional, and the Central. The Cordillera Central includes the highest mountain in the West Indian region, the 10,417-foot-tall Pico Duarte. In keeping with its place within the tropic zone, the country enjoys a mild climate with national mean temperature staying at 77°F and rarely rising above 90°F. The land offers a varied vegetation and has proven adaptable to cultivation of a wide variety of crops.

## THE NATIVE INHABITANTS

In 1492 when the Spanish caravels commanded by Admiral Christopher Columbus successfully ventured across the Atlantic, initiating the conquest and colonization of the island, the land was home to a thriving Taino society with a population of approximately half a million inhabitants. Scholars have traced the ethnic origins of the Tainos to a migratory wave of Arawak groups from South America that lasted several centuries. By the year A.D. 700 Taino culture and society had evolved with well-defined characteristics. The society Columbus found in 1492 had an economic structure built around fishing, farming, and hunting. Politically, the island was divided into five confederate tribes headed by caciques. The family structure followed a mostly monogamous organization, and the number of children per nuclear family varied from three to five. While the father exercised central authority, consistent with a patriarchal family structure, inheritance and succession followed a matrilineal model (Moya Pons 1995: 18–21).

## THE CONQUEST

During his first encounter with Antillean aborigines, Columbus perceived them as "well-built, with handsome bodies and fine features." Upon seeing the Admiral and his men, they appeared very pleased and became so friendly that it was a wonder to see. "Afterwards they swam out to the ships' boats where we were and brought parrots and balls of cotton thread and spears and many other things" (Columbus 1990: 29). Columbus had already sailed through the Bahamas and Cuba before December 5, 1492, when he arrived in Hispaniola. He decided to establish the Spanish settlements of the newly found territory on this island because of its promising gold deposits, which he and his entourage deduced from the fact that some of the aborigines wore golden ornaments. The Spaniards built there their first fort, called La Navidad, prior to the full colonization process. The thirty-nine Spanish soldiers who staffed the fort perished at the hands of Taino warriors, in retaliation for a rampage of rape and abuse of Taino women perpetrated by the Spaniards during the admiral's absence, when he made his first return trip to Spain to inform the Crown about his magnificent "discoveries."

Then followed a turbulent period of violence and depredation during which the native population was decimated as Spanish settlers spread throughout the island. A census of the colony taken in 1508 showed that a mere 60,000 Tainos remained from the nearly half a million found by the Spaniards in 1492. By 1519 they had shrunk in number to 30,000, and no available evidence exists to suggest that any pockets of Taino communities had survived by the end of the sixteenth century. They died from hunger, alien diseases brought by the colonizers, and the overall harshness of their forced labor in the gold mines set up by the Spanish. As historians affirm, "pregnant women systematically aborted or killed their own children to prevent them from becoming slaves" in the *encomiendas*, a system whereby the native population was proportionally allocated as property among the white settlers (Moya Pons 1995: 34). On the whole, Hispaniola flourished as the first Spanish colony of a region which the Europeans viewed as the New World. In time, it became the center of the entire Spanish colonization of the Western Hemisphere. Colonizing expeditions headed for Mexico, Peru, and the other mainland territories had to use Hispaniola as their point of departure. As the colony further developed it became known as Santo Domingo, after Saint Dominic, the Castilian founder of the Order of Friars and Preachers in the thirteenth century. The members of the order were known as the Dominicans, and centuries later the inhabitants of Santo Domingo would adopt that name for their republic.

## THE AFRICAN POPULATION

The decimation of the aboriginal population of Santo Domingo produced an acute need for slave labor, which the Spanish settlers sought to supply through the importation of captive workers from elsewhere. As a result, Santo Domingo became the port of entry for the first African slaves who arrived in the New World. When in 1501 King Ferdinand and Queen Isabella appointed Nicolás de Ovando as the new governor of Santo Domingo, they authorized him to bring "black slaves" to the colony. Ovando's fleet arrived in the island in July 1502, marking the start of the black experience in the Americas. Thenceforward, the black population in Santo Domingo grew dramatically. The Spanish Crown overruled a decree that permitted the importation of only those black slaves, who, born to a Spanish master, had received a Christian upbringing, allowing from 1511 onward the traffic of slaves directly from Africa.

As sugar-cane cultivation and sugar manufacture supplanted the mineral economy of the colony after 1516, the black presence on the island reached unforseen proportions, especially since the new industry drew its labor force almost exclusively from African slaves. Soon the black population outnumbered the white by a wide margin. A 1606 census assessed a differential of 1,157 white settlers versus 9,648 blacks, a numerical disparity that would continue to increase as the influx of Africans grew while the white Spanish settlers, disillusioned at the slim prospects for accumulating wealth, began to opt for emigration. By 1739 Archbishop Alvarez de Abreu was able to assess that of the 12,259 people who inhabited Santo Domingo the majority were "free blacks," which had a decisive impact on the ethnic composition of the population.

## ROOTS OF DOMINICANNESS

The year 1605 has been often cited as a pivotal moment for the earliest vestiges of the Dominican people. In that year, having failed to contain illegal commerce between their subjects and the merchant ships of Spain's European rivals, the colonial authorities decided to burn down the areas most directly involved in the violation. Governor Antonio Osorio personally supervised the work of setting the island's whole western band on fire, having first forced the residents to vacate the region. The flames, of course, eventually cooled off, and the vacant territories became a sort of no-man's-land, until marauders of various kinds began to make use of them. The area became a favorite hideaway for pirates, filibusters, and buccaneers. Subsequently, ambitious entrepreneurs would join them, primarily French ones, and by the end of the seventeenth century the western band of the island of Santo Domingo was filled with French-owned plantations that made intensive use of black slave labor.

Spain lost control of the western lands of the island, where a contiguous French colony developed in the course of the seventeenth century. The French colony became known as Saint Domingue, and by September 1697 the Spanish acknowledged the contiguous colony and increased trade with their neighbors, encouraged by the Peace of Ryswick signed between France and Spain. By the end of the following century, Spain proved unable to sustain its colonial share on the island, causing it to relinquish jurisdiction over the entire island to France by means of the 1795 Treaty of Basel. On the western side of the island, slaves rebelled against their French colonial masters, leading eventually to the black-ruled Republic of Haiti proclaimed in 1804 by a former slave, General Jean Jacques Dessalines. The fact that the newly liberated Haitian space had to share the island with a society that remained under European colonial rule became a source of tension between the eastern and western peoples of Hispaniola. First in 1801 and later in 1822, Haitian leaders sought to safeguard their independence by unifying the entire island under their rule. The second time, the unification period lasted twenty-two years, until the tie was broken by the success of a Dominican independence movement. On February 27, 1844, the Dominican Republic was proclaimed as a sovereign nation.

The fact that Dominican independence, the formal emergence of Dominicans as a people, occurred as a separation from the black republic of Haiti, and that racial self-differentiation has subsequently been used in nationalist discourse, has added levels of complexity to the racial identity of Dominicans, inducing in the population a reticence to affirm their own blackness openly despite the overwhelming presence of people of African descent in the country (Torres-Saillant 1995: 110). At the same time, the Dominican Republic is at the core of the Caribbean historical experience despite the fact that it is seldom viewed along with the other members of the West Indian family. What is now the Dominican land witnessed the first settlement of Europeans, the first genocide of aborigines, and the first cohort of African slaves in the archipelago. Santo Domingo initiated racial mixture, religious syncretism, linguistic nativization, and the overall creolizing process that typifies Caribbean culture. With the splitting of Hispaniola into two distinct colonial spaces that in time became nations with their own distinguishing characteristics, a complex process of historical evolution was set in motion. The harsh meeting of races and cultures that took place in the Dominican land during the colonial period was compounded later by the influx of French, German, U.S. black, Anglophone West Indian, Arab, Jewish, Canary Islander, Chinese, Cuban, Puerto Rican, and Haitian immigrants, all of whom, in varying degrees, have contributed to the ethnic and cultural formation of the Dominican people.

## PRECARIOUS AUTONOMY

Paradoxically, the Dominican Republic, like Haiti, stands out as one of the earliest Caribbean territories to attain its national independence. Yet, like Haiti also, it has often had its sovereignty threatened by foreign forces as well as by the self-interest of its political elite. Following the proclamation of the country's independence and the founding of the republic, the conservative element invariably outsmarted the liberal patriots, as may be gathered from the fact that Juan Pablo Duarte, the ideological architect of the independence movement, remained in exile until his death, never having had the opportunity to partake of the new nation's governing bodies. Ruled by leaders more committed to serving themselves than to the harsh labor of consolidating an independent and egalitarian society, the Dominican Republic suffered the annexation of its territory to the colonial domains of the Spanish Crown in 1861, only seventeen years after the nation came into being. The selling of the country's sovereignty by the conservative elite, represented then by President Pedro Santana, and the formal military occupation of the land by Spanish soldiers gave rise to the War of Restoration, a nationalist armed struggle that lasted until July 1865, when the invading army completed its withdrawal, having suffered defeat at the hands of Dominican nationalists.

On December 8, 1865, Buenaventura Báez, who had been president before and had a record of annexationist leanings, assumed the presidency.

Shortly thereafter, President Báez began modifying the constitution to give himself autocratic powers and implemented economic measures that favored his allies while severely harming the tobacco industry of the Cibao region. His government met with opposition from a liberal sector represented by General Gregorio Luperón, who had excelled as a liberator during the War of Restoration. Báez had to resign the presidency the following year. The next two years were marked by political disarray in the country. Rivalries among the leaders led to a series of short-lived governments, each of which confronted the armed opposition of rebel forces, culminating in the installation of a triumvirate which, apart from unleashing a reign of terror against liberal opponents, brought Báez back from exile and named him president.

President Báez took office again on May 2, 1868, beginning six years of repressive, corrupt, and autocratic rule. During that time Báez tried feverishly to annex the Dominican Republic to the United States and to sell or mortgage portions of the Dominican territory to foreign capitalists. After treating the country as a personal hacienda between 1868 and 1874, the shrewd caudillo had to resign following the armed opposition of a sector that enjoyed popular support. The old dictator, however, had not exhausted all of his tricks, and he came back to power in December 1876, implementing again a corrupt, repressive, and autocratic government that lasted fourteen months. The fall of Báez was followed by a trying political period during which the leaders of the liberal sector were able to establish their control of the Dominican government until 1886.

From 1886 to 1899, Dominicans endured the cunning and tyrannical rule of Ulises Heureaux, who ruined the country's economy and put it at the mercy of foreign governments and firms, a situation that led to the virtual control of the Dominican Republic by the United States. The takeover of Dominican customs in 1905 and the military occupation of the country from 1916 to 1924 clearly showed the United States as the small country's overlord. The bloodthirsty, corrupt Rafael Léonidas Trujillo, who perpetrated thirty years of tyrannical rule against the Dominican people, benefited greatly from the U.S. presence in the country. Not only was he himself a graduate of the National Guard, a military police force created by the U.S. marines during the occupation, but his totalitarian government was able to achieve absolute control of the whole society thanks to the disarmament of the civilian population and the centralization of the armed forces implemented by the U.S. military government.

The period following the death of Trujillo in 1961 marked a turning point in Dominican history, although the political resilience of Joaquín Balaguer, who occupied the presidency several times from 1966 to 1996, recalled the malevolent craftiness of Buenaventura Báez. Balaguer was Trujillo's puppet president in 1961, when the dictator met his death. When the formal dictatorship fell, Balaguer did his best to stay in power by feigning a disposition to embrace democracy, but he had to flee the country in 1962. Supported by the United States, the Catholic Church, the still active military elite of Trujillo, and the Dominican oligarchy, he managed to take power as president again in 1966, reelecting himself repeatedly through 1978 and again from 1986 to 1996, until he decided to strike a deal with the opposition party, Partido de la Liberación Dominicana, whereby he helped its candidate Leonel Fernández become elected.

Balaguer proved the equal of Báez in the corruption, repression, and autocracy of his governments, which largely brought back the worst vices of nineteenth-century Dominican politics. For the first time in history, Dominican society experienced a massive and contiguous exodus of people from the working-class, poor, and peasant sectors of the population. For the first time a diaspora was formed with a significant presence in Europe, the Caribbean, and the United States. As a result of the sequence of events unleashed beginning in the early 1960s, future historians looking at the Dominican people in the latter half of the twentieth century will have to widen their scope to include not only those on the eastern two-thirds of the island of Hispaniola but also those large masses of emigrants currently living in various other parts of the world.

Dominican flags waving during a community parade. © Josefina Báez.

# 1

# *U.S.-Dominican Relations: An Age-Old Romance*

## THE REDISCOVERY OF DOMINICANS

In the sweltering New York summer heat of July 1992, the United States had occasion to witness an instance of Dominican upheaval. A young man had died in the lobby of his own building at the hands of a police officer in Washington Heights, a Manhattan neighborhood populated predominantly by immigrants from the Dominican Republic. Rumors that painted the incident as a case of police brutality spread quickly, and many angry area residents took to the streets to protest what they at first understood to be an affront to the community. Three days of disturbances and social disobedience followed. Television and the print media flooded the nation with scenes featuring exacerbated demonstrators defying law enforcement agents. The spectacle of burning car tires and trash containers along Broadway and St. Nicholas Avenue terrified observers. The luminous flames came too soon after the riots incited by the Rodney King case in Los Angeles.

To add to the gravity of the situation, many feared that the uprising would grow to the point of tarnishing the Democratic Convention scheduled to take place in New York a few days later. A social explosion featuring Dominicans was threatening to disrupt the national convention of one of the country's two main political parties. It seemed conceivable that the Dominican community could shake a milestone in the mainstream political life of the United States. Responding to the panic that ensued, the police commissioner, many elected officials, and the mayor himself tried their best to appease Dominicans. The mayor consoled the family of the young man who had lost his life and gave his word that the city would hear the community's complaints and urged area residents to trust that justice would be done in case of verifiable wrongdoing on the part of the policeman in question.

By the third day the pacified demonstrators went back to their homes and allowed the courts to have the final say. Official reports concluded that the shooting had occurred in self-defense while the officer was wrestling with the young Dominican, whom police sources identified as a drug peddler. The court cleared the officer of the charges against him, and nothing happened in Washington Heights as a result of that decision. Despite expectations and warnings to the contrary, peace prevailed. But one thing became clear. For better or for worse, Dominicans as a community had made their entrance into the cognizance of contemporary Americans. Municipal authorities in New York City, for instance, learned important lessons about the overwhelming presence of Dominicans in town. They also learned about some of the problems besetting that community: overcrowded schools and apartments, distrust of the police, high rates of unemployment, a thriving drug trade, and widespread poverty. An article appearing in the *New York Times* over a year after the outbreak pointed to those socioeconomic conditions as constituting the "roots of Washington Heights violence" (D. González 1993: B1, 34).

## DOMINICAN FAMILIARITY WITH THE UNITED STATES

Americans who are students of their country's past in relation to the other nations of the Western Hemisphere did not need the July 1992 occurrences in Washington Heights to become aware of the presence of Dominicans. Their awareness of the long history between the United States and the people of the Dominican Republic would render the belated discovery superfluous. The dynamics that explain the large Dominican presence in the United States explain also the predominance of things American in the Dominican Republic. American values, institutions, consumer products, and popular culture formed part of the daily diet of Dominicans long before any consideration of traveling to the United States as immigrants or visitors might have crossed their minds. Pepsi Cola, Colgate, and General Electric, for instance, have been second nature to Dominican consumers for a long time. Santo Domingo, Santiago, San Pedro de Macorís, and other major cities in the country have streets and avenues bearing the names of George Washington, Abraham Lincoln, and John F. Kennedy, among other famous American statesmen. The country's national sport is baseball, an American game, and the population entertains itself with moving images on television and film, the majority of which comes from the United States.

## AMERICAN IDEAS AND THE BIRTH OF THE DOMINICAN STATE

The mutual attraction of Dominicans and the United States is not a twentieth-century phenomenon. It actually precedes the birth of the Dominican Republic as an independent nation. Perhaps the earliest indication of American influence among Dominicans occurred in the realm of political ideas dating back to the first half of the nineteenth century. On December 1, 1821, José Núñez de Cáceres (1772–1846), a distinguished functionary of the Spanish colonial government of Santo Domingo, released a separatist manifesto that proclaimed the political independence of the colony. In announcing to the world the emancipation of the Spanish-speaking inhabitants of the island of Hispaniola from the government of Madrid, Núñez de Cáceres embraced many of the principles and the rationale of the liberal Constitution of Cádiz, Spain, issued in 1812. But his text also echoed the language and the thinking of Thomas Jefferson as put forth in the Declaration of Independence promulgated on July 4, 1776, by the thirteen states of the United States of America.

The closing of the Dominican proclamation bears an unmistakable resemblance to the earlier American document. In the declaration penned by Núñez de Cáceres, the separatists did "declare and solemnly publish" the birth of their new nation as a "free and independent State," thereby absolving the colony of any obligation to the Spanish government; in the north, the signatories of the 1776 declaration stated: "We . . . solemnly publish and declare . . . these United Colonies . . . to be Free and Independent States," thus rendering them "absolved from allegiance to the British Crown." The Dominicans avowed their "full power and faculty to establish the form of government most suited to them, contract alliances, declare war, conclude peace, negotiate commerce agreements, and perform all the other transactions and treaties that are the rightful due of free and independent states" (*pleno derecho y facultad para establecer la forma de gobierno que mejor le convenga, contraer alianzas, declarar la guerra, concluir la paz, ajustar tratados de comercio y celebrar los demás actos, transacciones y convenios que pueden por derecho los demás pueblos libres e independientes*), in defense of which privileges they vowed to sacrifice their "lives, fortune and honor" (*nuestras vidas, fortuna y honor*) (Núñez de Cáceres 1992: 218). Their decree obviously resonates with vocabulary and clauses taken from the text espoused by the American Continental Congress in 1776, whose leaders had asserted their "full power to levy war, conclude peace, contract alliances, and to do all other acts and things which independent states may of right do," and they too had pledged "our lives, our fortunes and our sacred honor" to protect their prerogatives.

Núñez de Cáceres and his associates did not contemplate the abolition of slavery in the sovereign state they claimed to have founded, just as neither the Cádiz constitution nor the American proclamation of independence had envisioned the rights of "life, liberty, and the pursuit of happiness" to extend to black slaves. It would seem that the Dominican manifesto of national liberation suffered from the same moral flaw as its American and European models. In fact, the separatist movement had no popular appeal, and it soon perished, hence the custom of historians to refer to it as "the ephemeral independence." The leaders had planned to bring the newly created country under the aegis of Gran Colombia, a continent-wide Latin American republic projected by the liberator Simón Bolívar, but their efforts to engage Bolívar proved futile (Balcácer and García 1992: 53–54). The apparent inadequacy of the fledgling nation to thrive without the tutelage of a foreign political structure may have prompted the involvement of the Republic of Haiti, the neighboring nation that occupied the western portion of the island of Santo Domingo, to view the control of the whole island as a political imperative.

A state created by former slaves who had turned against their masters and defeated a large army sent by Napoléon Bonaparte to restore slavery and the old colonial order, Haiti had existed as an independent nation since 1804. But the young republic continued to live in fear of foreign invasions by powerful European nations that begrudged blacks in the Americas the right to rule themselves. Sharing the same island with a weak state such as that led by Núñez de Cáceres, which seemed unable to withstand European aggression, made Haitian sovereignty vulnerable. Haitian leaders feared primarily further French attacks. In addition, the Haitian government saw the annexation of the eastern territory as a solution to some of its own internal economic and political problems. Thus, the government resolved to unify the whole island of Hispaniola under Haitian rule and sent an army of 12,000 soldiers across the border. On February 9, 1822, the government of Núñez de Cáceres having abdicated, the ruling Dominican Creole elite awaited the Haitian chief of state Jean Pierre Boyer "at the gates of Santo Domingo to accompany him to city hall and the cathedral where they rendered him honors as President" (Moya Pons 1995: 124).

The unification period lasted twenty-two years, a period Dominican historians call "the Haitian domination." At first, the majority of the population in Spanish-speaking Hispaniola welcomed the change of government (Moya

Pons 1972: 34–36). Among the popular measures implemented by the Haitian ruler was the abolition of slavery and the elimination of racial privileges in Santo Domingo. Boyer's commitment to black liberation manifested itself also in the invitation he extended to free blacks in the United States to migrate to Hispaniola. Apart from providing the opportunity to enjoy full citizenship rights, which they could hardly hope for in the racially stratified American society, the Haitian president offered them "free passage, land, and temporary support while establishing themselves," an offer which many found attractive: "the first boatload arrived in the city of Santo Domingo in 1824, and by the end of the next year some 6,000 had immigrated" (Holm 1989: 504). Many of those who came fell victim to typhoid fever, causing some to return to the United States, but a considerable number stayed, and they settled, on the Dominican side of the island, in thriving communities, especially Samaná and Puerto Plata.

One gets a glimpse of the visibility of the U.S. black immigrants from the words, in late 1869, of the American adventurer Joseph W. Fabens who, in describing the population of Samaná, spoke of "both native Dominicans and those of American descent," adding his favorable impressions at having there attended religious services conducted by "the chaplain Reverend Jacob James" (cited in Welles 1966: 381–82). In 1870, when American observers visited Samaná, they assessed the black immigrants "to be a prospering community of approximately 600 members." Over one hundred years later a scholar who studied them spoke of "a considerably numerous group of English-speaking blacks" whose ancestors "came to this country almost 140 years ago" (Hoetink 1974: 9, 3). A linguistic survey carried out in Samaná during the 1980s found that 50% of the sample selected spoke English, which attests to the survival of the cultural forms and traditions of the descendants of the black Americans invited by Boyer (Holm 1989: 505). The same can be said of their adherence to the Wesleyan Methodist Church, a London-based house of worship brought by those immigrants in the nineteenth century. At the same time, a good share of the descendants of those immigrants had accommodated themselves to the way of life of the native Creole population both in rural and in urban settings. That would seem to be the case particularly with those living in Puerto Plata, where roughly 2,000 black Americans settled originally, according to a scholar who has studied them (Ortiz Puig 1978: 7, 153).

The end of the unification period came on February 27, 1844, when a Creole Santo Domingo elite that had managed to rouse some popular support proclaimed their separation from Haitian rule, thus giving birth to the Dominican Republic as an independent sovereign nation. Their declaration, entitled "Manifesto of the Residents of the Eastern Part of the Island Formerly Known as Española or Santo Domingo on the Causes of their Separation from the Haitian Republic," dated January 16, 1844, shows, even more clearly than the text of Núñez de Cáceres some twenty-two years earlier, the influence of American political ideas on the minds of the elite. The opening sentence should suffice as an illustration: "A decent attention and the respect owed to the opinion of all men and civilized nations demand that, when a people that has been united to another, should wish to reassume their rights, to claim them back, and dissolve their political bands, they ought to declare, with frankness and in good faith, the causes that move them to the separation" (Bobadilla, et al. 1992: 219). The reader will easily recognize these words as a lightly recast rendition of Jefferson's beginning in the American Declaration of Independence: "When in the course of human events, it becomes necessary for one people to dissolve the political bands which have connected them with another, and to assume, among the powers of the earth, the separate and equal station to which the laws of nature and of nature's God entitle them, a decent respect for the opinions of mankind requires that they should declare the causes which impel them to the separation."

The document whereby the first Dominican statesmen told the world about the emancipation of their nation from Haiti and its coming into being as a sovereign republic was sprinkled with language and ideas borrowed from the American experience. It is not surprising, therefore, that the country's first chief of state, General Pedro Santana, should yearn for recognition by the United States and by the great European powers. Such recognition would enhance the country's credibility commercially and diplomatically at the international level, without which the newly born Caribbean republic would have little chance of surviving in the world economic system. When approached by a Dominican envoy to Washington, D.C., the administration of President John Tyler hesitated at first but showed sufficient interest. In December 1844, Secretary of State John C. Calhoun suggested to the Spanish minister in Washington that the United States, France, and Spain should proceed to "recognize the new Republic, as a means of preventing the further spread of negro influence in the West Indies" (Welles 1966: 76).

## AMERICAN AGENTS IN SANTO DOMINGO

The Dominican question came before the Tyler administration toward the end of the presidential term, leaving little time to take action. It fell to President James K. Polk, inaugurated in March 1845, to follow up on the issue. The new secretary of state, James Buchanan, appointed an American agent in Santo Domingo, John Hogan, with the mandate of assessing the newly born nation. Having arrived there in December 1845, Hogan reported favorably on the general condition of the country, highlighting the racial composition of the population, which he estimated to be 230,000 inhabitants, as follows: 100,000 Caucasians, 40,000 Negroes, and the rest mulattoes (Welles 1966: 77). Race appeared particularly important to the American agent, as was the defense of the Dominican territory from Haitian encroachment. Haitian rulers did not at first resign themselves to the separation brought about by the Dominicans, and they made successive attempts to regain the eastern side of the island. As a result, sporadic armed confrontations between Haitian and Dominican forces took place until 1855.

The likelihood that the Dominican Republic might become a protectorate of a European power worried the United States government from the start of the nascent state. Spurred by the news of a Spanish protectorate then under consideration by Dominican leaders, Secretary Buchanan sent another envoy, Francis Harrison, as commercial agent to the Caribbean country. Harrison arrived there in March 1847, but, unfortunately, he died of yellow fever a few months later. Agent Jonathan Elliot soon came to replace him. The new agent did much to incite direct American involvement in Dominican affairs, as one can gather from a May 2, 1849, letter to Buchanan in which he enticingly informed the secretary of state about a conversation in which the Dominican chief of state, President Manuel Jimenes, had brought up the possibility of annexing the country to the United States (Welles 1966: 92–93).

The next U.S. secretary of state, John M. Clayton, who served under President Zachary Taylor, showed a greater degree of determination in regard to Dominican affairs. He appointed Benjamin E. Green American commissioner in Santo Domingo. The commissioner set to work speedily on advancing his country's interests, and his very first letter to Secretary Clayton discussed the possibility of acquiring the Samaná Province for the United States in exchange for "giving notice to the Haitians that they must cease to molest this people" (Welles 100). Green insisted further that Haitian aggression had given "force and universality to the feeling in favor of the whites in the Dominican Republic" (Welles 103–4). Green's line of thinking regarding the necessary involvement of the United States in Dominican life did not fall on deaf ears in Washington. In January 1851, President Millard Fillmore, who had become the U.S. chief of state following the death of President Taylor, appointed Robert Walsh as special agent specifically to go to the island of Hispaniola and prevail upon the Haitian government to desist from menacing Dominicans. The new secretary of state, Daniel Webster, had read in a letter from Commercial Agent Elliot that Dominican sovereignty depended on the United States to survive since the interference of the English aimed exclusively at "the protection of Haiti" to secure their own economic interests in Haiti and to advance their policy "to sustain the negroes in the Antilles" (Welles 111–12).

The American commitment to having a say in Dominican affairs became intensified with the coming into the picture of Secretary of State William Marcy, a strong believer in the need for his country to expand territorially, during the administration of President Franklin Pierce. While serving as the governor of New York, Marcy had befriended General William L. Cazneau, an adventurer and a veteran of the Texas war. Once in Washington, Marcy named Cazneau envoy to Santo Domingo in November 1853. The shrewd envoy, who met several times with President Santana, convinced Marcy of the great opportunities for accumulating wealth that Americans had in the Antillean nation. Urging Marcy to pursue a strong Dominican policy on the grounds that the country possessed rich natural resources that awaited development by the United States, Cazneau managed to receive a presidential appointment as special agent of the United States in the Dominican Republic on July 17, 1854 (Tansill 1938: 176–77). Cazneau got Marcy interested in negotiating a treaty that would lead to the acquisition of Samaná Bay for a U.S. coaling depot. He produced a draft of the projected treaty and the secretary of state approved it, authorizing him to follow it up with Dominican authorities. Along with Cazneau came Captain George B. McClellan, who rushed to survey the bay, inciting the angry suspicions of Spanish, English, and French diplomatic officers who already had denounced American ambitions in the country.

Opposition to Washington's Dominican plans came from the United States as well, chiefly from public opinion sectors that defended the interests of slave states that trembled at the thought of granting official U.S. recognition to the Dominican Republic. The New York *Evening Post* sought to discredit Secretary Marcy's schemes by publishing a "genealogy" of Dominican political leaders on September 2, 1854. The information in the genealogy meant to reveal that "the Dominican leaders were all either negroes or mulattoes, and that the pure white population of the Dominican Republic was almost a negative quantity," thereby alerting "Southern statesmen" as to the implications of extending privileges to a government "based upon negro or mulatto supremacy" (Tansill 1938: 181). While favorable voices did come to the fore, on the whole Cazneau and Marcy's plan failed to exact sufficient backing in the United States. Nor could the Santana government succeed in quelling the vigorous opposition generated at home. Thus, on September 9,

1854, the Dominican chief of state informed the U.S. special agent that the signing of a treaty could not take place until such time as the strong objections of the European powers could be swayed (Tansill 1938: 180; Welles 1966: 150).

The American commercial agent, Jonathan Elliot, continued to play a visible role in promoting his country's interests as well as in repelling the anti-American sentiments spread by the Spanish, French, and English consuls in the republic. In fact, Acting Commercial Agent Jacob Pereira barely escaped falling victim to an anti-American rabble roused by the Spanish minister Antonio María Segovia (Welles 1966: 173). Elliot continued to keep Secretary Marcy abreast of local events and to beseech that the American government retain its interest in the Dominican territory.

The protean character of General Cazneau enabled him to remain influential with the U.S. government through various administrations. He was reappointed special agent when President James Buchanan took office. In his official capacity, the Texan tried his best to earn the favor of the new secretary of state, Lewis Cass, for General Santana, who had just helped depose President Buenaventura Báez. Writing on behalf of Santana on April 7, 1859, Cazneau stressed that with the present ruler, "the Cabinet, Congress and the Courts are filled by white men," in contrast to the manner of a Báez whose party "aims at placing the supreme control in the hands of the negroes." He, in fact, insisted that the return of Báez would lead to the annexation of the country to Haiti and the empowerment of "blacks from the class most bitterly opposed to American interests" (Welles 1966: 200–201). Cazneau had more than diplomatic reasons to wish for Santana to receive the blessing of Secretary Cass and to uphold his racial argument. He and his partner, the enterprising adventurer Joseph Warren Fabens, who had also fought in the Texas war, owned a generous plot of land that Santana had granted to them for launching the project of a colony to be populated by citizens migrating from the United States to the Dominican Republic.

## AMERICAN IDYLLS IN THE DOMINICAN LAND

The entrepreneurs behind the projected American immigrant settlement in the Dominican territory had luring things to say regarding the virtue of the Caribbean country. Their portrayals typically echoed the images evoked by W. S. Courtney's book *The Gold Fields of Santo Domingo* (1860), which presented the reader with a pastoral landscape awaiting domination by American genius. The text undertakes to uncover, "exclusively in the interests of humanity," the uncharted realm of a "new Eldorado," namely, "the vast

mineral, agricultural, manufacturing and commercial resources of the Spanish part of the Island of Santo Domingo," having found it "scarcely credible
that such vast wealth, and especially mineral wealth, should have lain there
so easily attainable, for so many years and almost within the suburbs of our
great commercial cities, without exciting at least the cupidity, if not the
enterprise of the Yankee" (Courtney 1860: 9). Courtney had no doubt that
Americans should view the treasure of the Dominican land as their rightful
entitlement: "The fact has become palpable of recent years, that if the colossal
resources of the Dominican part of the Island are ever fully developed, and
rendered subservient to the interests of humanity as well as to the certain
and abundant opulence of those who undertake it, it must be done by the
Anglo-American" (11). The author reassured his readers that in pursuing the
riches that the Dominican land had to offer, one need not worry about native
Dominicans themselves. He highlighted the utter lack of "thrift and industry" in the natives, their politeness, courtesy, and affability, plus their dis-
interest in the "allurements of wealth," feeling no envy or resentment at
seeing "the man of industry and application . . . enriching himself at every
stroke" (132–33, 138).

The Civil War broke out in the United States in 1861, and the administration of President Abraham Lincoln had no time to devote attention to
Dominican affairs. But the relative detachment of the U.S. government gave
added impetus to private entrepreneurs, particularly since the president favored the idea of facilitating the colonization of emancipated blacks in the
West Indies or Liberia. A bill introduced on December 16, 1862, by Senator
Wilson of Massachusetts to abolish slavery in the District of Columbia passed
with an amendment that provided financial assistance in the colonization of
former slaves who desired to emigrate from the United States. The bill enlarged the potential clientele for the American colony conceived by Cazneau
and Fabens, who in 1861 had formed in New York the American West India
Company to stimulate migration to the Dominican Republic. The company's prospectus declared the ownership of extensive lands near the Ozama
River in the capital city of Santo Domingo, a fertile area deemed favorable
"for the introduction of a large number of agricultural homeless laborers
from the United States for whom the United States government feels a responsible interest and who would find there a most desirable home" (cited
in Welles 1966: 314).

While the United States was passing through the devastating Civil War
experience, the Dominican people had to suffer the surrender of their country's sovereignty to the Spanish Crown. The authoritarian President Santana
engineered the annexation in 1861. But the loss of Dominican independence

did not deter Cazneau and Fabens from pursuing their colonization project. A book published in New York by Fabens under the title *In the Tropics* paints the new colonial domination in placid colors. Writing in the second year of the annexation, the narrator says that the country now "possesses guarantees of personal liberty, to subjects and aliens, white and black, that cannot be questioned or set aside by any future rulers under the Spanish Crown, as these guarantees form part of the conditions of its annexation" (Fabens 1863: 304). Fabens' book, which would go through a second edition ten years later, purports to narrate the experiences of a young man after having lived as a settler in Santo Domingo for a period of twelve months. He tells, of course, a success story in order to seduce those workers who "are seeking new homes in countries where *intelligent* labor can best be made to supply the want of capital" (302). The author gives an enticing inkling of the kind of labor force that settlers might find in the receiving society, should they need native hands, by describing a laborer of his named Juanico: "He is the most patiently industrious Dominican I have yet seen, and by no means wanting in the capacity to learn and appreciate the use of improved implements of agriculture. His nature is single-minded, docile, and faithfully affectionate, and he is prized by me rather as an humble friend than a paid servant" (287).

In the first passage quoted from his book, Fabens refers specifically to the racial openness of the Spanish authorities, which insinuates an interest on his part to appeal equally to whites and blacks in promoting the American colony of Santo Domingo. Another publication, a pamphlet published at around the same time, stressed particularly the relaxed attitude toward race prevailing in the Dominican Republic. Aiming to provide a brief overview of the country, the pamphlet says this: "In the tropical countries, as a general rule, no austere prejudice against color prevails. Somehow the climate softens us, and the 'embrowned children of the sun' are not looked upon with that shrinking repugnance manifest in the more frigid social system of the North" (*Santo Domingo* 1863: 10). The publisher of the pamphlet, the American West India Company operated by Cazneau and Fabens, makes the connection clear. Here too the American entrepreneurs seemed committed to presenting the Dominican Republic as a transracial society in order to engage as wide as possible a constituency in their colonization project.

## BRINGING DOMINICANS INTO THE UNION

The annexation of the Dominican Republic to Spain ended on July 11, 1865, with the departure of the last Spanish troops, defeated by the nationalist Restoration army after three years of bloody war, a few months after the

American Civil War had come to an end, with the soldiers of the North having preserved the Union against Southern secession. Secretary of State William H. Seward, who had served under President Lincoln and was being kept on the job by President Andrew Johnson, cast his eyes on Samaná Bay as a desirable spot to install a naval base to remove the danger of any further European aggression in the Caribbean. On January 15, 1866, he and his son Frederick Seward, who was serving as assistant secretary of state, arrived in Santo Domingo to meet with President Báez. When the meeting took place, Cazneau and Fabens served as interpreters. The assistant secretary of state pursued a commercial treaty with the Dominican government, for which he would return to Santo Domingo in the company of Vice Admiral Porter of the U.S. Navy. Seward's terms for the treaty were thought by many patriots to compromise national sovereignty, but, through the intervention of American Commercial Agent J. Sommer Smith, President Báez agreed to sell the Samaná Peninsula to the U.S. government in May 1868.

Secretary Seward had little difficulty in securing concessions from President Báez, but influential nationalist spokespersons protested loudly against the prospect of selling or leasing a portion of their territory. Though tempted by the negotiation with Báez, who had expressed his willingness to annex the whole republic if the U.S. government rewarded him appropriately, Secretary Seward expected serious obstacles in getting the treaty ratified by the U.S. Congress. Previously he had failed to obtain ratification for the sale of the Danish West Indies. As a result, negotiations went no farther than a recognition by President Johnson, included at length in his Fourth Annual Message to Congress, on December 9, 1868, that Americans should consider that "the time has arrived when even so direct a proceeding as a proposition of an annexation of the two Republics of the island of Santo Domingo would not only receive consent of the people interested, but would give satisfaction to all other foreign nations" (cited in Welles 1966: 355).

The next American president, General Ulysses S. Grant, seems to have taken the recommendation of his predecessor very seriously. He sent his private secretary, General Orville E. Babcock, to the Dominican Republic as commissioner to negotiate the annexation. In Santo Domingo, Babcock allied himself with Cazneau and Fabens, who had become ardent proponents of annexation. The three of them from then on insisted on reassuring President Grant and Secretary of State Hamilton Fish about the presumed joy of Dominicans in general concerning the prospect of becoming a territory of the United States (Tansill 1938: 383). In truth, however, the annexation negotiations made Báez a very unpopular president, hence the favor enjoyed by such leaders as General Gregorio Luperón, who headed an armed resistance against the government. At times, American warships had to intervene in support of Báez, a practice that was denounced by U.S. Senator Charles Sumner, a foe of the annexation project, who chaired the Senate Committee on Foreign Relations. Speaking in Congress, the senator brought this into the open: "Báez is maintained in power by the naval force of the United States, and that, being in power, we seek to negotiate with him that he may sell his country" (Sumner 1969: 272).

The obstinacy with which the Grant administration sought to acquire the Dominican territory manifested itself in a retaliatory attitude even to American officers who hesitated to support the plan. Commercial Agent J. Sommer Smith lost his job when he, in correspondence with Secretary Fish, criticized the maneuvers of Cazneau, Fabens, and Babcock (Tansill 1938: 400). Major Raymond Perry, appointed in his stead, communicated in writing to Fish his reservations about a plebiscite whereby President Báez purported to demonstrate that Dominicans would enthusiastically welcome a change of sovereignty. Dated June 1, 1870, Perry's letter attests to the violence, coercion, and intimidation used by President Báez to produce results that suggested popular support for the annexation (cited in Welles 1966: 386). His antagonism to Báez, and the aversion he inspired in Cazneau, Fabens, and Babcock, caused Major Perry to fall from grace with President Grant and Secretary Fish, who permitted him to resign a few days later.

The debate over the annexation project in the United States, just like the scheme to bring Americans to settle in the Dominican Republic some years before, generated idealized images of the Dominican land and its people. Among the authors whose writings aimed to make annexation palatable to public opinion sectors weary of having their Union joined by other races and cultures was American journalist Deb Randolph Keim. Following a trip to Santo Domingo, Keim published a book that presented the Dominican people as a tribe of noble savages that went about their ways undisturbed by modern concerns. While granting that "rivalry of race, black, mixed, and white, in politics and governmental affairs, has led in many cases to trouble and violent contention," he assured his readers that there "distinction of color, in social life, is entirely unknown" (Keim 1870: 168). Finally, although President Grant had insisted in a message to Congress that "the acquisition of Santo Domingo will furnish our citizens with the necessaries of every day life at cheaper rates than before," the opposition to the plan did not die out either in the Dominican Republic or in the United States.

Realizing the great obstacle posed by the vigorous opposition championed by Senator Sumner, President Grant settled for securing Senate approval to send to the Dominican Republic a commission of inquiry to assess the con-

dition of the Caribbean country and its people in order to help Congress
ascertain the desirability of acquiring the new territory. The commission,
made up of Senator Benjamin F. Wade, Senator Andrew D. White, and
Senator Samuel G. Howe, arrived in Santo Domingo on January 16, 1871.
The commissioners prepared a formal report of their observations there
which concludes, in sum, that "the physical, mental, and moral condition of
the inhabitants of Santo Domingo was found to be more advanced than had
been anticipated" (*Report of the Commission of Inquiry to Santo Domingo*
1871: 13). The findings of the commission pleased President Grant who felt
confirmed in his efforts to bring Dominicans under the U.S. flag. Speaking
to Congress on April 5, 1871, he insisted that "indeed, it is confirmed by
the report that the interests of our country and of Santo Domingo alike
invite the annexation of that Republic." Yet, the commission's findings did
not attract all the legislative backing that the president needed. The report
did not result in any action, and Grant ceased his annexationist effort. By
the same token, soon thereafter, Cazneau and Fabens "removed themselves
from the Dominican scene" (Welles 1966: 400–401).

## DOMINICAN BLACKNESS AND FREDERICK DOUGLASS

Opposition in the United States and the serious challenge posed by nationalist insurrections against President Báez in the Dominican Republic put
an end to the political measures that made the Dominican land "almost a
territory," to echo the title of a book that studies the attempts made at
annexation (Nelson 1990). Following the failure of the scheme, American
statesmen showed during the next two decades little interest in things Dominican. For that time the country seemed to disappear from American
political discourse. Samuel Hazard, who had traveled to Santo Domingo with
the commission of inquiry in 1871, wrote only two years later about the
oblivion into which the Dominican Republic had fallen in the public opinion
sectors of the United States (Hazard 1873). Perhaps the most salient feature
of the rapport between the two countries at the time was the U.S. government's choice of black Americans to serve as diplomatic representatives in
the Dominican Republic. President Rutherford B. Hayes, who succeeded
President Grant in the White House, appointed a black man named H. H. C.
Astwood American consul in the Dominican Republic, a position that he
occupied through the first years of President Grover Cleveland's first term
in office (1885–1889). The choice arguably entailed a recognition of Dominicans as a people of color who would welcome a black diplomatic official,
thus marking a change from the former racial characterizations of Dominicans by American observers.

The administration of President Benjamin Harrison brought to the Dominican Republic the renowned Frederick Douglass, the most notable black American living at the time. The Dominican ruler, General Ulises Heureaux, had for some years urged the U.S. government to establish a diplomatic mission in the country, particularly since one already existed in Haiti, where Douglass served as the American minister in Port-au-Prince. Heureaux's request was finally granted when the famous black human rights activist and author arrived on February 23, 1890, as the first American chargé d'affaires in Santo Domingo. President Heureaux, who stands out in Dominican history for his shrewd autocratic grip on Dominican society for fifteen years, was a black man. He often appalled negrophobic whites who could not concede to a black person the ability or the right to rule a country. Irrespective of the merits of any criticism of his political conduct as a despotic president, they too often stressed his blackness in a sense that seemed to racialize his actions. One such commentator, Sumner Welles, a chief of the Latin American Division of the Department of State who in the 1920s went to the Dominican Republic as envoy extraordinary and minister plenipotentiary, ascribed to Heureaux the weaknesses "of the savage—his domination by his sexual passions, which were never satiated, and his lust for blood" (Welles 1966: 449). Welles affirmed that Heureaux "was ever mindful of the completely negroid aspect of his face, which he attempted to mitigate so far as Nature made it possible by resorting to the most elaborate uniforms, to the most immaculate clothes" (1966: 449).

The texture of Welles' remarks would seem to construe blackness as a condition for which one needed to compensate. When Douglass met the black Dominican chief of state, however, he did not think that his physical features required palliation. Nor did Douglass find it necessary to adduce genetic bases to explain the president's psychopathology. He noted, on the contrary, the President's superior intellect: "Besides his native language he speaks French and English, the latter remarkably well. He is a man of energy and intelligence and his history proves him to be well versed in statesmanship" (Douglass, cited in Welles 1966: 447). Consistent with Douglass' background as a fighter against racial oppression, he assessed the physical and mental attributes of Heureaux in terms that differed radically from the racially deprecatory portrayal of negrophobic white observers such as Welles.

## DOMINICANS IN AN AMERICAN PROTECTORATE

The dictatorship of Ulises Heureaux from 1886 through his death in 1899 was marked by the Dominican government's unscrupulous borrowing from various foreign states and private corporations. In addition to causing the country's growing indebtedness, the president made risky concessions to foreign capitalists, including Americans, mortgaging major tracts of lands and natural resources. In March 1893 the San Domingo Improvement Company began operating with a group of New York financiers. Headed by Smith M. Weed and Charles Webb, with the support of John Wannamaker, a Cabinet member in the administration of President Benjamin Harrison, the company came into being with the purpose of buying up all of the Dominican Republic's international debts in exchange for a contract that included the leasing of Samaná. The advent of the San Domingo Improvement Company, an enterprise that promised handsome profits to the investors involved, gave the United States unprecedented influence over the country's financial activity. New York broker firms attained virtual control of the booming sugar industry in the republic, and the company began to direct the management of Dominican custom receipts. In addition, President Heureaux "granted the Clyde Steam Lines Company an exclusive monopoly over the transportation of passengers and freight between New York and Santo Domingo," marking "a growing influence of the United States over Dominican economy and finances" to the detriment of "European interests that had traditionally dominated Dominican commerce" (Moya Pons 1995: 272).

The death of President Heureaux in 1899 began a turbulent period in Dominican history marked by a scramble for power among various political factions. The country's political disarray threatened to harm the interests of American investors, including the San Domingo Improvement Company, and Washington found it expedient to seek to regulate matters through direct involvement in the country's political and economic affairs. The United States expressed particular concern about the threat made by various European governments to intervene militarily to collect debts in the Dominican Republic. It was, in effect, the Dominican situation that catalyzed the Corollary to the Monroe Doctrine, a famous foreign policy pronouncement disclosed by President Theodore Roosevelt through a letter read on his behalf at a dinner given in New York City on May 20, 1904. Roosevelt's letter states in essence that the United States has the right—the obligation even—to intervene directly in the affairs of any of the nations of the Western Hemisphere as a result of wrongdoing or disorder. "If a nation shows that it knows how to act with decency in industrial and political matters, if it keeps order and it pays its obligations, then it needs fear no interference from the United States," stipulated the American president (cited in Munro 1964: 77).

Roosevelt's corollary found immediate application in the establishment of a customs receivership in the Dominican Republic under the direct supervision of American officials to make possible a general adjustment of foreign claims. In 1905, during the administration of President Carlos F. Morales Languasco, who enjoyed American support and showed considerable willingness to heed the directives of the United States, President Roosevelt put into effect a so-called modus vivendi, a provisional fiscal arrangement whereby Washington took over the collection of the Dominican customs at all ports of the country. To that end, Colonel George R. Colton, a retired officer of the U.S. Army, who had done similar work in the Philippine customs service, became general receiver and collector of the Dominican Republic (Munro 1964: 94, 106). The U.S. Senate had yet to approve the action taken by the president in the small Caribbean nation. A treaty that would formalize the measure of direct management of Dominican financial life still awaited ratification in the Senate, where legislators once more weighed the question of whether the United States should meddle in the Dominican land.

In keeping with the debate among legislators in Washington, Dominicans again gained currency in American public discourse. Various publications that appeared at the time attest to the eagerness with which certain opinion sectors sought to garner public favor for the president's Dominican policy. An overview of the Dominican Republic that appeared in New York in 1906 illustrates this argument:

The importance of our relations with Santo Domingo was realized many years ago by President Grant, when he tried to annex that Republic to the United States, and again by President Roosevelt, when he framed the treaty referred to above. The advantage of President Roosevelt's policy over President Grant's is that the treaty affords us the opportunity of removing the probability of European intervention without assuming the burden which annexation would impose upon us. (Anon. 1906: 1)

The anonymous author quotes Samuel Hazard approvingly to the effect that Dominicans are "an honest and inoffensive people, among whom, in rural districts, a person may travel alone and unarmed all over the country with treasure without danger" (1906: 19). The writer also concurred with his source's description of the racial characteristics of the people in question: among Dominicans "white blood preponderates" in contrast to the Haitian population, among whom "the black race is in complete ascendancy" (18–19). The previous year, an author writing about the country in a similar vein affirmed that Dominicans "are, with very few exceptions, white," asserting further, "The division of the island into two countries was owing to the difference of race and refusal of the white Dominican to be governed by the black Haitian" (Hancock 1905: 50). The insistence of depicting Dominicans as white would seem to emanate from the desire to make them appealing to a society that still upheld white supremacist beliefs.

## AMERICANS GOVERNING DOMINICANS: 1916–1924

President Roosevelt's temporary modus vivendi, which eventually received Senate approval on February 25, 1907, became the formal treaty called the Dominican-American Convention, which thenceforward legitimized Washington's control of Dominican finances. The arrangement would remain in effect until 1940. While the American receivership came into existence as an attempt to solve many of the country's problems, in effect it served as an initial phase of the sociopolitical development that less than a decade later would culminate in the official installment of an American military government in the Caribbean country. Despite the presence of a foreign overlord, the clashes among the various political factions that vied for supremacy continued, exacerbated at times by the Dominican government's failure to command respect given its inability to allocate public funds freely and its subservience to American overseers. By August 1914, the Dominican situation so troubled the administration of President Woodrow Wilson that U.S. officials convened many of the most active and prominent political leaders in the Dominican Republic to present them with what became known as the Wilson Plan. Essentially a political ultimatum, the plan urged the contending factions to lay down their weapons and to select a provisional government that all would find suitable. Should they fail to agree on a provisional president, the United States would appoint one and give him military support to check insurgents. Among the duties of the temporary government would be holding an election which the United States would monitor closely. If the successful candidate met with the approval of the United States, Washington would support the new president and help him eradicate armed opposition (Munro 1964: 292). The Dominican political leaders reluctantly accepted the American proposal.

The Wilson Plan, which worked relatively well, resulted in the election of President Juan Isidro Jimenes, whose government held the country together for nearly two years. However, in early 1916, when Jimenes was faced with a rebellion led by the very influential military leader General Desiderio Arias, he adamantly refused to request the direct intervention of the American armed forces that were insistently offered to him, preferring to resign instead, which he did on May 7, 1916. Since Arias was deemed a foe of U.S. interests in the country, Rear Admiral W. B. Caperton received orders to march into the capital to expel the rebels and restore order. Declaring a state of occupation, the American authorities from that point onward decided not to recognize, even to allow, the rise of any Dominican chief of state who did not beforehand pledge to accept American economic and political guidance. Fearing, above all, that permitting further Dominican elections might lead to the selection of an anti-American political faction, President Wilson "reluctantly" authorized Secretary of State Robert Lansing to proceed with a formal military invasion. Thus, on November 29, 1916, Captain Harry S. Knapp proclaimed the military occupation from his flagship *U.S.S. Olympia* in the port of Santo Domingo. The captain dissolved the Dominican government and began an American military rule of the country that would last until 1924.

A book written two years into the invasion by Judge Otto Schoenrich, an American observer, celebrated the achievements of the military government as a virtual salvation for the country. Despite the sadness that Dominicans might naturally feel "at passing under the government of a foreign power," the author contended that "the independence of the Republic has long been a fiction, that real freedom is only now beginning to dawn, and that American assistance will give the greatest impetus to prosperity" (Schoenrich 1918: 392). With the continuance of close ties between the two countries, preferably in the form of a protectorate, Judge Schoenrich envisioned boundless progress for the occupied territory. He saw American tutelage as an agent of "peace and efficient administration," which would generate "the multiplication of roads, railroads and other public improvements, the extension of education and a rapid advance of the people and the development of the country," turning the Dominican territory into "one of the richest gardens of the West Indies" within "a few years" (394).

Less sanguine analyses of the intervention, enjoying the privilege of historical distance, include a book written by Melvin M. Knight, published in a series entitled "Studies in American Imperialism" four years after the end of the occupation. In it, Knight portrayed that chapter of U.S.-Dominican relations as an illustration of military power used in the service of capitalist accumulation for private investors (Knight 1928). Several decades after Knight's book was published, a major study of the subject, written by Bruce Calder, focused primarily on native resistance to the occupation and concluded with a characterization of the American intervention in the Dominican Republic as "a policy neither wise nor just, a policy basically unproductive for all concerned" (Calder 1984: 252). Nor was the occupation without opposition in the United States while it was taking place. The Dominican question, which elicited heated debates at the time, became a hot issue in the presidential election of 1920, which brought the Republican Warren G. Harding to the White House.

President Harding's secretary of state, Charles Evans Hughes, played a crucial role in resolving the hurdles that had kept American troops on Dominican territory for a longer time than had originally been planned. Hughes prevailed upon a group of distinguished Dominican leaders to accept a plan whereby the country's government would go back to Dominican hands while Washington remained in control of the customs receivership. To that end, the former chief of the State Department's Latin American Division, Sumner Welles, was appointed American commissioner by President Harding. Once in the country, the commissioner succeeded in forming a Committee of Representatives out of the leadership of the diverse constituencies that hoped to rule the nation following the evacuation of U.S. troops. The members of the committee agreed to name a provisional government with the mandate to organize a national election. After a series of mishaps, and thanks to the active involvement of the American commissioner, the temporary government was installed and a popular election took place, bringing victory to General Horacio Vásquez, the candidate with the most popular appeal among Dominicans at the time. With the native government of President Vásquez in place, the withdrawal of the occupying forces followed, and on September 18, 1924, the last U.S. Marines left the Dominican Republic, putting an end to eight years of direct American rule.

## DOMINICANS AMERICANIZED

By the time the United States relinquished the command of the Dominican state to a native leadership, the country and its people had undergone significant change. The Americans left a new and comprehensive highway system that improved transportation and communication. The number of available schools and the size of the student population had increased dramatically. Besides education, major strides had been made in sanitation, health, and public works. Governmental institutions had become more stable as a result of the successful disarmament of the civilian population accomplished by the American military government. But less felicitous changes also had occurred. The constabulary created by the Americans, which had mastered the techniques of repressing dissent by means of force, organized now as a national police, responded with blind discipline through its own hierarchy to the central government, and could be used against the people. In the economic realm, the military government's predilection for the sugar industry made the country dependent on a fluctuating world sugar market and gave preeminence to foreign investors who had been attracted to the Dominican Republic by the abundance of cheap lands. The favor extended to foreign-dominated economic enclaves largely ruined small business and family operations. The avalanche of U.S. goods that poured into the country following the promulgation of the Tariff Act of 1919, which granted American products duty-free passage into the Dominican market, proved overwhelming for local producers. By the same token, the propagation of U.S. trademarks, from cars to clothes to foodstuffs to toys, induced in consumers a strong partiality toward American products, which is perhaps most clearly illustrated in the fact that American baseball replaced cockfighting as the national sport (Moya Pons 1995: 336–38). In short, among the enduring legacies bequeathed by the U.S. military government was the widespread Americanization of taste in Dominican society.

## THE DOMINICAN EXODUS

The Dominican Republic did not become "one of the richest gardens of the West Indies" as the good Judge Schoenrich had so enthusiastically predicted. On February 23, 1930, an uprising orchestrated by the chief of the armed forces, General Rafael Leónidas Trujillo, a trainee of the American constabulary who had moved up the ranks through devious means, brought democratic progress to a halt. By exerting a tremendous influence over the military, now a powerful institution that, with the civilian population disarmed, held a virtual monopoly over violence, General Trujillo forced his way into the presidency and began thirty years of the bloodiest reign of terror that Dominicans had ever experienced throughout their history. At crucial points during the first years of his rule, the dictator benefited from the expert guidance of the U.S. armed forces, as documented by the Dominican scholar Bernardo Vega in his book *Trujillo y las fuerzas armadas norteamericanas* (1992). Vega has also mapped the rapport between the United States and Trujillo in over ten other volumes on the subject. The historian Dana Munro, thinking of Trujillo's case, reasons that "the evolution of the constabularies was a disappointment to those who hoped that they would help to promote republican government" (Munro 1964: 540).

Trujillo's autocratic regime would come to an end only with his assassination in 1961, which was followed by a brief period of joy at the prospect of freedom and democracy for the Dominican people. In December 1962, Dominicans went to the polls and elected as their president an anti-Trujillo leader who had come back from exile, Juan Bosch. Bosch belonged to a liberal Latin American leadership associated with reform, social justice, and democratic ideals. However, his government was met with the unbending hostility of the corporate sector, the remnants of Trujillo's military oligarchy, and the Catholic Church, which collaborated in bringing about the president's overthrow only seven months after his inauguration as the constitutionally elected chief of state. Political turbulence and social disruption ensued. Conservative provisional governments succeeded each other, and an armed insurrection against the illegal regime brought many young patriots to their deaths in 1963. Subsequently, on April 24, 1965, a liberal wing of the armed forces rose up in arms, demanding the return to legality and the constitution. The people took to the streets in support of the insurgents, who became known as *constitucionalistas.* The forces of the people got to the verge of proclaiming the victory of their patriotic cause when, on April 28, 1965, American soldiers marched into the country, sided with the conservative flank of the war, and helped defeat the *constitucionalistas.*

The American invasion of 1965 crushed the Dominican people's hope of grabbing the reins of their own political destiny. Juan Bosch, who went into exile following the coup, was allowed to return, not to occupy the presidency to which he was entitled constitutionally as would be done decades later in the case of deposed Haitian president Jean Bertrand Aristide, but simply to run for office along with other candidates. Bosch was to compete with Joaquín Balaguer, the last of Trujillo's puppet presidents, who had vowed to continue the tyrant's legacy while saying his eulogy before the dead body of the dreadful ruler. A favorite of the conservative sectors, the military, and the United States, Balaguer had the resources of the state put at his disposal during the campaign. Bosch, on the other hand, had to endure a series of terrorist operations launched against his party, the Partido Revolucionario Dominicano (PRD), by the Trujilloist army officers, emboldened by the military presence of the United States. The PRD had "more than 350 of its activists . . . killed between January and May 1966. Bosch himself was not allowed to go out of his house to campaign and had to address his constituency in daily speeches broadcast through the radio" (Moya Pons 1995: 390). As could be expected, Balaguer won the elections, and on June 1, 1966, he became president of the republic for the second time. The return of Balaguer, whose economic restructuring and development policies increased unemployment and underemployment as well as salary depression; the brutal persecution unleashed by the conservative government against revolutionaries; and the promulgation in the United States of the Immigration Law of 1965, which made it easier for Third World people to secure American visas, combined to propel a massive, growing, and continuous exodus of Dominicans from their native land. It also happened that, whereas the Trujillo dictatorship had sought methodically to prevent emigration, the Dominican government now seemed bent on encouraging it.

A Dominican crowd during a festive activity. © Eduardo Hoepelman, courtesy of CUNY Dominican Studies Institute archives.

# 2

## *Escape from the Native Land*

### A CONTINUOUS EXODUS

Massive emigration from the Dominican Republic began in 1962 after the death of dictator Rafael Leónidas Trujillo. The dictatorship had severely restricted international migration. Only diplomats and a handful of well-to-do people of unquestioned loyalty to the government were granted visas. Some authors have argued that Trujillo's restrictive emigration policies sought to prevent disgruntled Dominicans from denouncing his government abroad (Frank Canelo 1982: 41). Moreover, his migration policies reflected a commitment to a population increase, which the state promoted in three ways: encouraging childbirth, sponsoring preferably European immigration, and discouraging emigration. The dictator believed that an increase in population would strengthen his regime. Thus from a mere 900,000 people in 1920 the Dominican population rose to 3 million inhabitants by the end of his rule (Cassá 1982: 572). The regime associated underpopulation with a shortage of laborers which presumably stalled economic development. Trujillo's government from the outset rewarded childbearing, along with European immigration, by offering incentives to large families, as a way to remedy the perceived scarcity of laborers (Moya Pons 1977: 516). Scholars concur that Trujillo's control of the population movement developed in response to the direct exigencies of a new productive system: "Policies restricting mobility within and off the island were formulated to ensure the supply of skilled workers to the burgeoning import-substitution industries of Santo

Domingo, as well as agricultural producers on whom the cultivation of traditional export and food crops hinged" (George 1990: 29).

But with the fall of the dictatorship, the number of Dominicans admitted
to the United States as permanent residents grew dramatically (see Figure
2.1), as can be illustrated by the 10,683 who arrived in 1963 in comparison
with the 4,603 who had arrived the year before. The momentum continued
from 1962 through the 1990s. From 1962 through 1972, the annual mean
of Dominicans who left their homeland for the United States was 11,445,
which increased to over 16,000 during the 1970s and to over 30,000 during
the 1980s. Since 1983 the number of permanent residencies granted to Dominicans has exceeded the limit of 20,000 persons per country set by the
Immigration and Naturalization Service (INS). In 1991 and 1992, the number reached over 40,000 each year. In 1991 the Dominican Republic ranked
third among countries where spouses of U.S. citizens received permanent
resident status and also third among the countries where over 50% of the
children of U.S. citizens abroad were born (*INS 1991 Statistical Yearbook*).
Both of these categories are exempted from quota limitations.

## WHO ARE THE IMMIGRANTS?

Understanding the causes of the massive Dominican migration to the
United States requires at least a minimal examination of the demographic
background of the migrants, particularly their social class status and their
regional procedure. The first scholars to study this phenomenon classified
post-1965 Dominican migrants as predominantly rural, uneducated, poor,
unskilled, jobless workers (González 1970, 1976; Hendricks 1974). In their
view, these migrants came to the United States in search of a solution to
their grave economic problems. A study published by researchers Antonio
Ugalde, Frank D. Bean, and Gilbert Cárdenas, however, challenged that
demographic picture. They argued, instead, that most of the migrants came
from the urban middle-class sectors of Dominican society and that they were
neither the poorest nor came from the ranks of the unemployed (1979: 243–
44). Contrary to the early scholars, who based their judgment on small ethnographic surveys of rural communities in the Dominican Republic, Ugalde,
Bean, and Cárdenas used a national survey on mortality covering 25,000
households and 125,000 people that the Ministry of Public Health and Social
Welfare had coordinated under the sponsorship of the United States International Development Agency. Given the prestige of the data analyzed by
Ugalde, Bean, and Cárdenas, their findings have influenced most subsequent
studies of Dominican migration to the United States.

## Figure 2.1
## Dominicans Admitted to the United States from 1960 to 1991

| Year | No. |
|------|--------|
| 1961 | 3,045 |
| 1962 | 4,603 |
| 1963 | 10,683 |
| 1964 | 7,537 |
| 1965 | 9,504 |
| 1966 | 16,503 |
| 1967 | 11,514 |
| 1968 | 9,250 |
| 1969 | 10,670 |
| 1970 | 10,807 |
| 1971 | 12,624 |
| 1972 | 10,760 |
| 1973 | 13,921 |
| 1974 | 15,680 |
| 1975 | 14,066 |
| 1976 | 12,526 |
| 1977 | 11,655 |
| 1978 | 19,458 |
| 1979 | 17,519 |
| 1980 | 17,245 |
| 1981 | 18,220 |
| 1982 | 17,451 |
| 1983 | 22,058 |
| 1984 | 23,147 |
| 1985 | 23,787 |
| 1986 | 26,175 |
| 1987 | 24,858 |
| 1988 | 27,189 |
| 1989 | 26,723 |
| 1990 | 42,195 |
| 1991 | 41,405 |

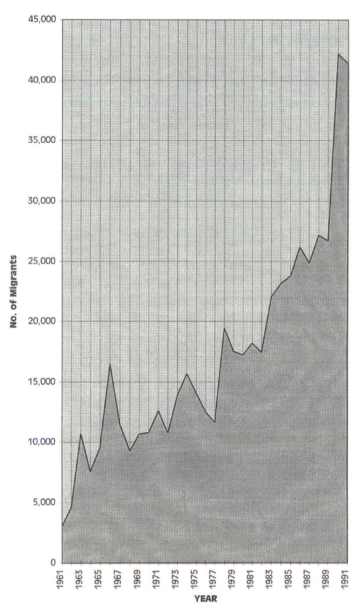

*Source:* INS Reports

However, as will become clear in the pages that follow, Dominican immigrants defy monolithic portrayals in their socioeconomic background at
home as well as in their present condition as an immigrant community in
the United States. They come from different class sectors, from rural as well
as urban origins, from uneducated as well as schooled contingents. The number of Dominicans who held jobs prior to migration—at whatever level of
gainfulness or status—probably competes with the number of those who
belonged to the ranks of the unemployed. Similarly, once located in the
United States, the socioeconomic continuum of Dominicans ranges from a
starving welfare recipient with dim prospects for obtaining productive employment to the spectacularly successful designer Oscar de la Renta, one of
New York's notable multimillionaires. To define the community one must
avoid drawing exclusively from the extremes (Hernández and Saíllant 1996:
30). However, there is no doubt that the majority of Dominican immigrants
in the United States are devalued workers owing to their low educational
attainments.

## THE MAKING OF A MIGRATORY MOVEMENT

Massive migration from the Dominican Republic developed in response
to the development policies put into effect after 1966. Statistics on patterns
of employment and sectorial production indicate that job loss and underemployment have systematically increased or remained high due to ill-advised
economic development strategies. These strategies have not generated enough
new jobs to produce an effective balance between supply and demand in the
labor market. They have also tended to accentuate the gap between the well-
to-do and the poor, resulting in an impressive economic growth along with
acute poverty and marginalization. In those circumstances, increasing accumulation implies the use of less living labor, with the resulting creation of
an enlarging pool of inactive workers. At the same time, the expansion of
accumulation entails the regulation of surplus labor, via emigration and low
birthrates, as well as the devaluation of employed workers through low wages
and reduced expenditure in social services and public institutions.

A massive migratory movement from a given society into another generally
occurs as a result of several variables. It does not depend entirely on the will
of the migrants. The movement of a large human contingent involves the
power structures of both the sending and the receiving societies. These may
or may not effectively safeguard their respective borders. Depending on the
specificities of the political moment, they may implement measures that seek
either to curtail or to foment a migratory flow. Irrespective of what exactly

may have activated the movement in question, or whether or not the home and the host countries have been completely aware of all its implications, it is unlikely that the mobility of people across national borders could develop without the consent, either formal or informal, of the gatekeepers of both societies.

## RESTRUCTURING THE DOMINICAN ECONOMY

Under Trujillo the Dominican Republic embarked on a development model based primarily on modernizing as well as expanding the agricultural sector and on developing an industrial complex. That model viewed the population as workers and consumers needed for the country's economic development, hence the effort to prevent emigration, including any unabsorbed contingent of workers who were perceived as a necessary surplus. An increase in agricultural production for both the internal and the external markets, particularly during the 1930s, was achieved thanks to a well-structured agrarian policy which favored the expansion of small-and large-scale farmlands. With the exception of sugar cane, agriculture rested mostly on the shoulders of peasants, many of whom had already lost their lands under the dictatorship or earlier during the North American occupation of 1916–1924 and were now available as hired hands (Cassá 1982: 118–31).

Similarly, the industrial production which developed in the urban centers, particularly in the city of Santo Domingo, depended on a readily available and mobile labor force. In the words of a prominent historian,

The industrialization that began during World War II and continued without interruption until 1960 altered the purely administrative character of Santo Domingo, converting it into a manufacturing center that attracted tens of thousands of Dominicans from the country and cities of the interior in search for jobs. . . . Lured by the hope of finding work in one of the new industries being built, they began to form an ample urban labor market that would supply Dominican industries with a cheap labor force in the years to come. (Moya Pons 1995: 376)

Indeed, the number of workers employed in the manufacturing industry, excluding sugar production, increased from 12,937 in 1950, to 18,787 in 1957, and to 24,021 in 1962 (Moya Pons 1992: 378). A similar growth took place in the expanded bureaucracy, the construction sector, the armed forces, and in newly created service agencies. Employment in the public sector increased from 40,476 in 1950 to 110,349 in 1962, and total employment grew from 87,747, to 195,887 during the same years (Moya Pons

1992: 378). Trujillo's economic model, in other words, relied heavily on the development of an integrated sectorial production and made intensive use of labor.

Following the demise of the dictator, the social democrat Juan Bosch became president of the Dominican Republic in December 1962 in an election that gave him over 60% of the popular vote. However, on September 25, 1963, after being in office for approximately seven months, his government came to an end through a military coup d'état. Collaborating in the overthrow were various forces of the Dominican elite, including merchants, the Catholic Church, landowners, and industrialists, who opposed many of the new government's policies of social reform and denounced Bosch as a Communist. A triumvirate made up of corporate executives and lawyers, whose cabinet consisted of right-wing entrepreneurs and lawyers with strong ties to big business, replaced Bosch (Moya Pons 1995: 383).

The largely unpopular triumvirate was confronted by constant civil unrest and demonstrations of social discontent. Finally, a civil war erupted, headed by a liberal faction of the military that called for the return of the constitutionally elected president. But the popular revolt triggered the direct intervention of the United States, whose troops invaded the Dominican Republic on April 28, 1965, to keep Bosch from regaining power, thus preventing the emergence of "another Cuba" in the region. President Lyndon B. Johnson sent 42,000 U.S. soldiers to the small Caribbean country ostensibly to save lives and protect U.S. interests in the country (Moya Pons 1995: 388). On September 3, 1965, after considerable struggle between the constitutionalist forces (those demanding a return to the constitution) and their opponents (Trujillo's army and the U.S. marines), the civil war ended with a peace treaty that established a provisional government under the watchful eye of the Organization of American States and the United States. The accord also stipulated a new presidential election for June 1966. Meanwhile, the U.S. marines remained in the country, and the Dominican military became reconstituted as a force directly under American command and fully "dependent on the U.S. government for the payment of salaries and the provision of clothing, food, munitions, and equipment" (1995: 390). A favorite of the United States, Joaquín Balaguer, the last of Trujillo's puppet presidents, easily won the election.

Under President Balaguer, the Dominican Republic embarked on a development project that privileged industry and commerce. The economic model drew on a heavy influx of foreign capital and the promulgation of economic policies that favored industrial and commercial expansion. One can argue that the nascent native bourgeoisie's commitment to furthering its wealth in the country created the necessary conditions to facilitate foreign capitalist accumulation in the Dominican Republic. At the same time, international investment from advanced nations of the world had a need to incorporate new lands for production, new workers, and new consumers to escape economic slowdowns and unionization and, most of all, to resist competition. It was the combination and the interplay of these factors, external and internal, that, in the end, created the conditions for a massive international migratory movement of Dominicans directed particularly toward the United States.

Balaguer took office on June 1, 1966, and by April 23, 1968, his government had already approved a new investment legislation, Law 299 of Industry and Incentives Protection, which thenceforward served as the basis for most capitalist accumulation in the country. Approval of the new law required intense negotiations among the different factions of the Dominican bourgeoisie. The government had clearly demonstrated its commitment to facilitate the accumulation of the private sector. But native capitalists wanted to ensure that, despite the entrance into the picture of foreign investors whom they saw as necessary and inevitable, they would control specific areas of production (Moya Pons 1992: 140–64). Law 299 offered enticing incentives, from complete exoneration or reduced tariffs, to the provision of infrastructures for the development of industrial complexes. The new law was also meant to prevent direct competition between foreign and national capital by funneling foreign investment to areas of production that could not be undertaken by the native corporate sector. This law fostered a tripartite model of accumulation composed of the government, the private sector, and international capital. Each one depended on the other two to sustain the newly established social order. This complex collaboration would prove decisive for massive Dominican migration to the United States.

## STABILITY, FAMILY PLANNING, AND EMIGRATION

Balaguer's firm political control of the country was vital for the success of the new economic plan. The government undertook a pacification campaign that included political repression, killings, incarcerations, and opening the doors to expel unwanted voices that antagonized the regime. Though no written agreement existed, the U.S. and the Dominican governments acted in unison. Political dissidents received visas to travel to the United States. Others would apply for a passport and the government would simply grant it. In 1959, 19,631 people applied for a passport and only 1,805 got one; in 1969, every one of the 63,595 petitions received approval (Frank Canelo

1982: 42). Through the abundant issuing of passports, the Dominican Republic tacitly encouraged emigration. The magnitude of the Dominican exodus after 1966 would suggest that the doors were opened to expel surplus labor as well as dissidents.

The encouragement of emigration as a way to ease a government's implementation of economic restructuring was not new. During the 1950s, for instance, Puerto Rico witnessed the emigration of thousands of people who left a society in the midst of industrial modernization. Scholars agree that by the early 1960s Puerto Rico enjoyed high economic growth as a result of an impressive industrial complex based on U.S. investment. However,

without emigration, the effects of that accomplishment on living standards would have been negligible. Between 1948 and 1965 Puerto Rico saw the unusual spectacle of a booming economy with a shrinking labor force and . . . shrinking employment. This seemingly paradoxical situation was made possible because migration reduced the labor force, while productivity gains were sought through an increased capital-labor ratio. . . . Estimates of the population siphoned off between 1950 and 1965 run from 900,000 to one million, including the children born abroad to migrants. (History and Migration Task Force 1979: 127–28)

Although the Dominican government did not acknowledge its strategy of encouraging emigration to reduce population pressure, sufficient evidence exists to show that, at the time, the size of the population was a matter of concern; it is clear from the firm control of population growth put into effect then. Shortly after Balaguer took office in 1966, a National Family Planning Program came into being. The program was integrated by the Asociación Dominicana Pro-Bienestar de la Familia (PROFAMILIA), an organization established in 1966 and financed by the U.S. International Development Agency and the Consejo Nacional de Población y Familia, a government office created in 1968 to support the efforts of PROFAMILIA.

The growth of family planning (FP) initiatives in the Dominican Republic has been dramatic. In 1968 only eight clinics offered FP guidance and services in the country. By 1985 this number had increased to 493, excluding the many community posts that dispensed contraceptives and the services offered in private clinics through special arrangements. Similarly, the number of women covered by FP services increased considerably between 1975 and 1986. Among women between fifteen and forty-nine years of age, the proportion of FP users rose from 20% to 31% from 1975 to 1986, and among women who were living with a man (married or not married), the proportion grew from 32% to 50% during the same years (Ramírez 1991: 31, 34).

By the same token, permanent sterilization has become the most popular contraceptive method used by women in the Dominican Republic. The use of contraceptive pills ranged from 5% to 9% between 1975 and 1986, but the frequency with which women had recourse to sterilization rose from 8% to 33% between the same years (Tactuk et al., 1991: 12). Statistics indicate that FP practices in the Dominican Republic have proved successful. After the 1960s, the fertility rate fell sharply in the country. The 1960 average of 7 children to every Dominican woman decreased to 3.7 in the 1985–1990 period (see Figure 2.2), placing the Dominican Republic among the four leading countries with the lowest fertility rates in the Latin American region. Actually, statistics predict that between the years 2025 and 2030, the Dominican Republic will have reached population stability.

The implementation of family planning in the Dominican Republic did not stem from a fear of overpopulation on the part of the Dominican people (Vega 1990: 260). It was part of a long-term U.S. foreign policy on population control, directed particularly at areas receiving U.S. investment. The Uruguayan thinker Eduardo Galeano has observed that

Robert McNamara, the World Bank president who was the chairman of Ford and then Secretary of Defense, has called the population explosion the greatest obstacle to progress in Latin America; the World Bank, [McNamara] says, will give priority in its loans to countries that implement birth control plans. Lyndon B. Johnson's remark has become famous: "Let us act on the fact that less than $5 invested in population control is worth $100 invested in economic growth." (Galeano 1973: 15–16)

They believed that some places in the world had too many inhabitants and their reproduction pattern was a matter of international concern.

As a result of this preoccupation of the United States, the Agency for International Development from 1968 to 1972 allocated an operating capital of 100 million dollars for FP initiatives in Latin America alone. By 1986 the Dominican Republic could boast of 4,000 FP workers charged with the task of disseminating new ideas about family size among the people. The poor, and women in particular, "learned" that their poverty had to do with their unchecked fertility and that they needed to remedy their biological behavior. The perception of poverty as an individual's problem, rather than a social issue, legitimized the condition of inequality in Dominican society and exonerated the state, the power structure, and the privileged social sectors from their share of responsibility in the country's inability to provide for all the citizenry.

**Figure 2.2**
**Dominican Republic Fertility Rates from 1950 to 2000**

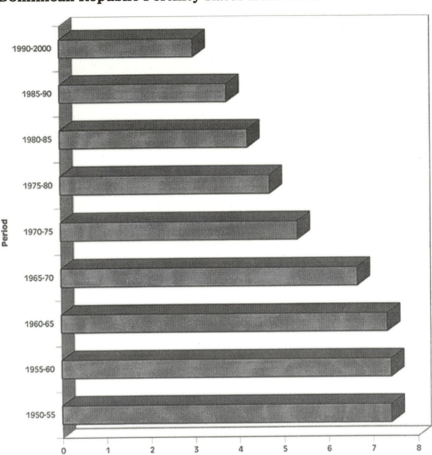

*Source:* Caram de Alvarez 1991: 52

The collaboration of the U.S. and the Dominican governments in the implementation of FP in the Dominican Republic suggests that both perceived population growth as a problem and both were interested in controlling it. Both governments, however, had different motives. To the U.S. government, the emigration of Dominicans was a short-term measure that aimed to resolve an immediate political problem, that is, the deportation of revolutionaries who might challenge the government of Balaguer and the new social order. To the Dominican ruling structure, the massive emigration of people seems to have entailed a long-term strategy whereby both political dissidents and excess workers would leave the country.

John Bartlow Martin, the U.S. ambassador to the Dominican Republic, played a key role in developing the channels for the Dominican exodus. Martin, who enjoyed respect in Washington, D.C., for his knowledge about the Dominican Republic, received his diplomatic appointment from President John F. Kennedy in 1962 as the first U.S. ambassador to the country in two years. Trujillo's 1960 assassination attempt against the president of Venezuela had led to a sanction of the Organization of American States against the country and suspension of diplomatic ties.

When Martin first met with the Consejo de Estado, a seven-member governing body that ruled the country temporarily after the dictatorship crumbled, the topics of discussion included violence in Santo Domingo and the granting of U.S. visas to Dominican troublemakers. In a lengthy book he wrote, Martin declared,

They [the Consejo] almost took rioting for granted—and no wonder: All last Fall and Winter they had lived with rioting. Trujillo's fall had cut loose long pent-up tensions, and the streets were chaotic. President Bonnelly said that well-trained Castro/Communist agents were paying thieves and hoodlums to riot. I asked if we could help. Reid and Bonilla Atiles immediately said yes—they wanted technical help in training the police to control riots, in setting up a secret anti-subversive unit to deal with Castro/Communists, and in arranging deportations. (Martin 1966: 8)

Having actually begun before Martin's arrival in Santo Domingo on March 9, 1962, deportations extended throughout his term:

By the end of the year we had some 125 deportees in the United States, most sent before I arrived. The riots mounted. Cautiously, the Consejo began to deport agitators under the Emergency Law. The Castro/Communists denounced it in the name of freedom. So did the political parties seeking the votes of the deportee's relatives. And we became involved—we had to issue U.S. visas for people that the Consejo deported to the United States. (Martin 1966: 99–100)

But the encouraged mobility of Dominicans to the United States was not limited to the deportation of "Castro/Communists." On a first trip to Washington since the beginning of his Dominican sojourn, Ambassador Martin spoke with the secretary of state about "the visa mess," by which he meant the increasing number of visa applicants in the Dominican Republic. Stationed daily in front of the American Consulate were long lines of people whom he believed needed to be served. The number of visa applicants grew to the point that it created a backlog in the outdated American Consulate.

Several months after his visit to the State Department, the ambassador reported, "We finally got what we needed—a new Consulate building at the Fairgrounds, far from downtown Santo Domingo, three extra vice consuls, and a new consul" (Martin 1966: 120). As a result, as noted by Christopher Mitchell, "the growth in Dominican migration in these years was one of the most rapid spurts in recent population movement from any Caribbean society. The administrative simplification and speedup initiated by the U.S. Ambassador surely contributed significantly to this high level of legal migration" (Mitchell 1992: 100). The official actions taken by Martin to facilitate the migratory process were motivated by the U.S. foreign policy which "sought (especially from 1961 to 1966) to limit political tensions in a nation where government instability was taken by Washington as an open door to radical revolution. . . . It is likely that administrative actions on migration were only loosely influenced by prevailing pro-Balaguer assumptions, rather than stemming from well-pondered choices in foreign policy" (1992: 90, 106).

Looking at the role of the United States in expediting the mobility of Dominicans to the North American mainland, it is probable that the strategy may have backfired, yielding in the long run unintended consequences and results. Although it stabilized a government preferred by the United States, the granting of so many visas also led to the establishment of immigrant settlements that would provide support systems, further fueling the massive mobility of Dominicans to the United States. The manifest purpose of granting visas to eliminate political opposition created a momentum that triggered the exodus of thousands of people in a migratory movement that has remained unabated to the present day.

## ECONOMIC GROWTH AND SURPLUS POPULATION

During Balaguer's first two presidential terms (1966–1974), the Dominican Republic witnessed an economic boom. Characterized by an economist as an "accelerated growth," the country's gross national product (GNP) showed a growth rate of 12.2% in 1969 and 12.9% in 1973. During the 1969–1973 period, the manufacturing sector grew at an annual rate of 14.7%, construction at 20.1%, and agriculture at 8 %, with industrial employment growing at an annual rate of 5.9% between 1970 and 1974 (Ceara

Hatton 1990a: 64–65, 70). Specialists agree that the economic boom was based on three interconnected variables: foreign investment, foreign aid, and the favorable prices exacted by Dominican products, particularly sugar, on the international market (Ceara Hatton 1990a; Calvo and Dilla 1986). Foreign capital entered the Dominican economy on a large scale: "The amount of money the United States poured into the Dominican Republic between 1966 and 1973 was enormous in proportion to the small size of the country's economy" (Moya Pons 1995: 397). Foreign aid, in the form of state loans, grants, or food supplies reached approximately $122 million between 1965 and 1966, $133 million between 1967 and 1969, and $78 million per year between 1969 and 1973 (1995: 397). Direct foreign investment, on the other hand, increased from $154 million in 1964 to $396 in 1972, with nearly 89% of that sum coming from the United States (Del Castillo et al., 1974: 183).

## MODERNIZATION AND IMPORT SUBSTITUTION

With the aim of modernizing the country to compete effectively in the international market, the Dominican Republic has since 1996 adopted various economic strategies. The first was import substitution (IS), a strategy developed in the 1950s that was recast during Balaguer's government through the passing of Law 299. This development model drew on the teachings of economist Raul Prebisch who had posited that underdeveloped countries could accomplish capitalist national development by limiting the level of imports and creating an industrial infrastructure for assembly or manufacture of pertinent goods internally. The application of that model generated a rapid expansion of the industrial sector in the Dominican Republic. Between 1970 and 1974, industrial production grew at an annual rate of 120% (Duarte and Corten 1982). Between 1970 and 1977, the capital invested in the food industry increased from DR$130.9 million to DR$196.8 million, and in the intermediary industry, from RD$31.2 million to DR$70.5 million (Vicens 1982).

But contrary to expectations, import substitution did not yield the desired results. It did not substitute imports, nor did it reduce unemployment. Importation of consumer-related manufactured products increased in almost every single industrial branch. From 1973 to 1980, imports of total manufactured products rose from 26.8% to 31.9%. Those years witnessed an increase in the importation of food, tobacco, and beverages from 7.5% to 9.8%, of furniture from 4.78% to 12.41%, of clothing from 13.48% to 22.76%, of shoes from 4.26% to 10.62%, and of paper from 31.32% to

**Table 2.1**
**Unemployment Rates (% of labor force)**

| Year | (%) |
|------|------|
| 1970 | 24.1 |
| 1973* | 20.0 |
| 1978* | 24.4 |
| 1979* | 19.3 |
| 1980 | 22.2 |
| 1981 | 20.7 |
| 1982 | 21.3 |
| 1983 | 22.1 |
| 1984 | 24.2 |
| 1985 | 27.2 |
| 1986 | 28.7 |
| 1987 | 25.0 |
| 1988 | 20.8 |
| 1989 | 19.6 |
| 1990 | 19.7 |
| 1991 | 26.6 |

*City of Santo Domingo only

1970–1979: *Source:* Ceara Hatton 1990b: 60.
1980–1991: *Source:* Ceara Hatton and Croes Hernández 1993: 18. Used with permission.

49.40% (Ceara Hatton 1990a: 80–81). At the same time, in 1970, the national population census reported an unemployment rate of 24.1%. Since then the rate of unemployment has not gone below 19.3 % (see Table 2.1).

Between 1970 and 1979, 305,600 able bodied men and women entered the labor force in the country, bringing the total number of employed workers in the industrial sector from 113,040 to 139,503, an absolute increase of 26,463 jobs over a period of nine years, creating an average of fewer than 3,000 new jobs per year. Thus, the direct transference of resources from the state to the private sector, as formalized through Law 299, did not significantly alter the internal structure of the industrial sector. It neither expanded the industrial sector's ability to incorporate new workers into the process of production nor heightened the level of industrialization in the country.

The economic strategy favored by the Balaguer regime called for the constant increase of technology over labor, which had a negative effect on the industrial sector's capacity to incorporate the labor force. In 1960, for instance, the creation of an industrial job required a capital investment of

DR$3,125, a sum which had risen to DR$5,000 by 1968, and would go over DR$9,000 in 1981. Similarly, between 1968 and 1981, a total of 678 new industries were approved under Law 299. These industries, holding an investment capital of DR$498,664, created only 54,891 new jobs, an average of 4,222 jobs per year. By 1981 industrial expansion still demanded less than 5,000 new workers per year at a time when the active economic population was growing at an annual rate of 5.5%, generating some 56,000 men and women ready to work every year.

## THE CATTLE-AGRICULTURAL SECTOR

The emphasis placed on the industrial expansion through the implementation of Law 299 of industrial incentives had an adverse effect on the development of the agriculture-cattle sector whose contribution to the GNP would decrease progressively. The agribusiness industry turned increasingly capital intensive, narrowing the space for jobs in the countryside and provoking the migration of laborers to the urban centers. In 1970 the contribution of the agriculture-cattle sector to the GNP represented 23.2%, with an annual growth rate of 9.8%. But this contribution began to decline, shrinking from 22.1% in 1971 to 16.9% in 1981. The agricultural subsector underwent a similar process of deterioration, reducing its contribution to the GNP from 16.1% in 1971 to 10.3% in 1981.

Another factor that has fostered unemployment is the use of large-scale farmlands (*latifundios*) which have traditionally undermined the use of Dominican labor, as can be seen in the examples of cattle raising and sugarcane production. Cattle raising, which requires the largest amount of land, does not employ many workers since the animals do not need constant attention. More important, cattle raising is extensive, and landowners tend to use between 10 and 15 *tareas* (a tarea = ⅙ of an acre) per animal. Sugarcane represents the second largest user of large-scale farmlands. Not only does it depend on seasonal production, but the sugarcane fields employ primarily Haitian immigrant laborers rather than Dominican workers.

## ECONOMIC CHANGES

In the mid-1970s the Dominican economy shifted from a production oriented mainly to traditional products (coffee, sugar, tobacco, and cocoa) to one centered around the development of free trade zones (FTZs), tourism, and nontraditional agricultural products. Traditional products began to lose popularity on the international market, particularly in the United States, as interest in other goods grew. Sugar, which had been the base of the Dominican economy, reduced its contribution to the GNP from an average of 25% in the late 1970s to about 8% in 1990, whereas tourism accounted for over 40% at the end of the 1980s. Although the change began to manifest itself clearly during the 1980s, when the contribution of the service sector to the GNP increased significantly, the shift may be traced to Balaguer's first government through his open-door policy to foreign investment.

Critics have argued that capitalist accumulation via foreign investment tends to deform the local economy, subordinating it to outside forces. The influx of foreign loans implies a series of commitments toward the lending institutions. As a Dominican scholar has put it, "These commitments imply not only the direct repayment of the loan, but also a number of dispositions related to economic development, subordinated to specific strategies designed by the international agencies, and the binding of the Dominican import market to the supply of goods produced by the lending countries" (Lozano 1985: 187–189). Besides, foreign capital hardly contributes to the diversification of the local economy since it normally targets areas of production for which an international market already exists (Del Castillo et al., 1974).

Foreign investment has affected the supply side of the Dominican market, which has become increasingly flooded with goods from the United States. In many cases, U.S. products are sold in the Dominican market at much higher prices than in the United States. Dominican retail stores carry products imported from the United States sometimes at three to five times their original U.S. price (Riley de Dauhajre 1995: 1). (See Figure 2.3.) The importation of these products fostered a new market configuration with its own consumers, showing positive results for the expansion of both international and native capitalist accumulation. The higher prices paid by Dominican consumers, the mobility of goods, and the new market demands that ensued all contributed to the expansion of industrial capital for both U.S. and native investors linked with the commercial as well as the import sectors. But the job markets remained dismal.

Foreign investment in the Dominican Republic occurred in the context of the reorganization of production by the United States and other advanced capitalist societies that sought to further their process of accumulation. This involved relocating capital and production offshores. Attracted mainly by a high number of unemployed people, low wages, and, most of all, fiscal prerogatives provided by the government, including large tax exemptions and a favorable monetary exchange rate, foreign capitalists rushed to the Dominican free trade zones. The first FTZ, with just one industry in operation,

# Figure 2.3
## U.S. Consumer Products in the Dominican Market (In RDS)

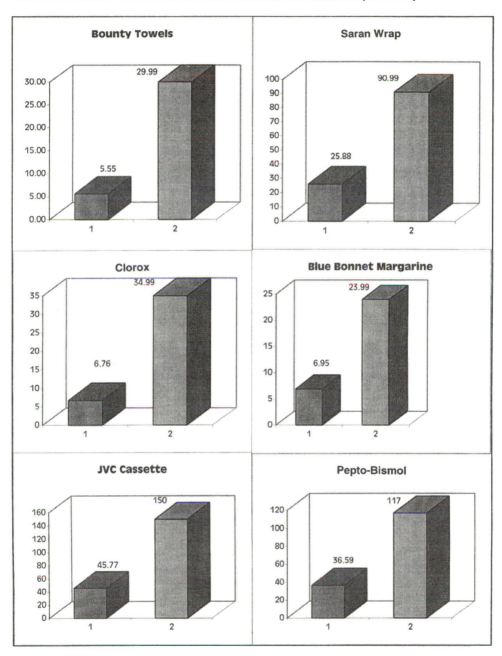

Key: 1=US
     2=DR

# Figure 2.3, continued

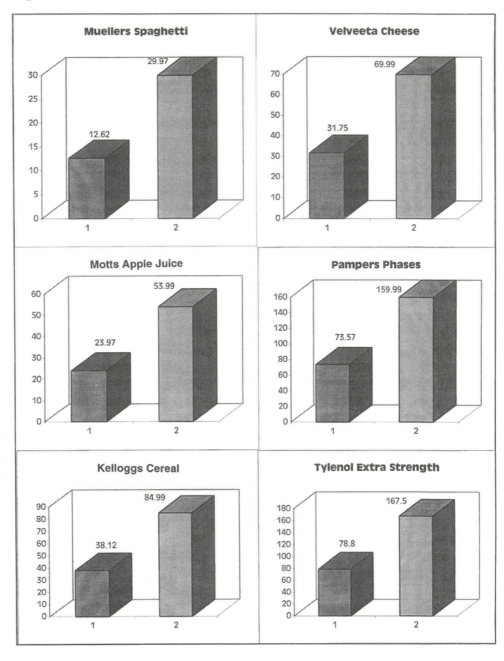

Key 1=US
  2=DR

50

# Figure 2.3, continued

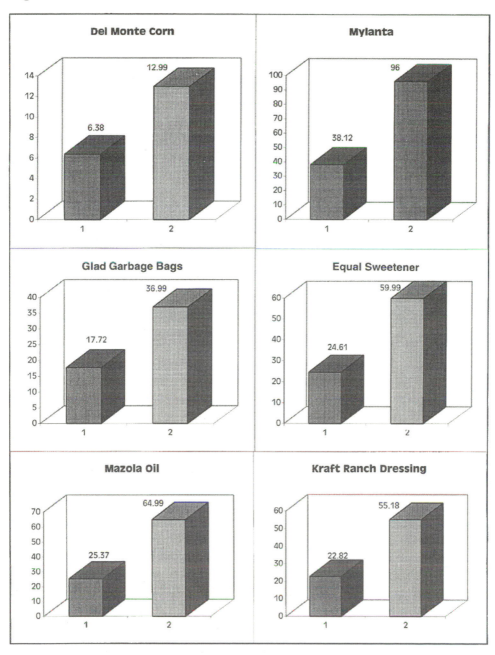

Key 1=US
　　2=DR

*Source:* Riley de Duahajire 1995: 1.

opened in the eastern city of La Romana in 1969, but by 1988 sixteen FTZs had spread throughout the country, with 224 industrial installations. The number of direct jobs created had increased from 504 to 85,000. By 1993 there were 462 companies operating in thirty FTZs in the country, yielding 164,296 jobs (see Table 2.2). By 1988, after Mexico, the Dominican Republic led the Latin American and Caribbean regions with the largest number of FTZ firms (Abreu et al., 1989: 68). But critics agree that, although the FTZs have generated badly needed jobs and revenues, they have not contributed significantly to the country's industrial development nor to alleviating the serious unemployment problem.

The FTZs employ only 3% of the Dominican labor force. Most workers are internal migrants, largely women, generally not unionized, who earn less than the national minimum wage (Gómez and Báez 1988). The recruitment of young women as the primary labor force and the high rate of turnover in the FTZ plants have contributed to an increasing level of unemployment among women (Sassen 1988: 97). One could argue that recruiting mostly young women has the effect of expanding the absolute size of the labor force and undermines the possibilities of the FTZs to alleviate the growing unemployment problem in the country. The composition by sex of the economically active population in the Dominican Republic reflects a tendency toward the "feminization" of the labor force. In 1960, for every 100 persons in the labor force, 11 were women, but by 1981, this number had increased to 29, and by 1983, particularly in the city of Santo Domingo, which is a frequent destination for migrants from the interior, the number had risen to 38. The FTZs have contributed significantly to the growing proletarization of women as have other areas of the expanded manufacturing subsector.

Tourism has undergone a remarkable growth during the last fifteen years. The amount of revenues generated by this subsector jumped from US$16.4 million in 1970 to US$616 million in 1988; tourism has become the single largest contributor to the national economy. But the growth of this industry did not reduce the need for emigration. Tourism contributed to increasing the level of importation in the country. The products it uses, from the beds, linen, and silverware to most of the food tourists eat, need to come from abroad. Moreover, tourism is a capital-intensive activity that uses skilled and semi-skilled labor, providing very little room for the employment of unskilled workers. In effect, although tourism has generated the largest amount of revenues in the GNP since early 1980, the number of jobs it has created has only modestly increased: from 10,800 in 1980 to 17,258 in 1987, and to 24,000 in 1989.

**Table 2.2**
**Evolution of FTZs in the Dominican Republic**

|  | 1975 | 1980 | 1985 | 1990 | 1993 |
|---|---|---|---|---|---|
| No. of FTZs | 3 | 3 | 8 | 25 | 30 |
| Industries | 29 | 71 | 136 | 331 | 462 |
| Jobs | 5,872 | 16,440 | 30,902 | 130,045 | 164,296 |
| Revenues in millions of US$ | 12.8 | 44.5 | 54.6 | 214.0 | 350.0 |

*Source:* Manzueta Martinez 1994: 2. Used with permission.

## ACCUMULATION AND CRISIS

The two development strategies implemented in the Dominican Republic since the end of the 1960s, namely import substitution and the export-led economy, have yielded equally questionable results. The first, emphasizing industrial production to reduce the level of importation of manufactured products, failed in its essential mandate. By 1978 it was obvious that the country was importing much more than it was producing and selling. Consequently, a growing deficit began to characterize the economy (see Table 2.3), and an increasing amount of money was borrowed from foreign institutions, disproportionately enlarging the country's debt, which went from US$290.6 million in 1970 to U.S. $3,844.9 million in 1988.

The second development strategy, the export-led economy, also proved ill-advised. By the end of the 1980s, the Dominican economy had essentially the same industrial coefficient as in 1968, when Law 299 was approved. The level of industrialization had not increased, and the intensification of industrial capital grew to the point that, by 1981, it took an expenditure of over RD$9,000 to create an industrial job. The economic policies of the Dominican Republic could not fix the balance of payment or reduce imports. At the same time, they could not stop the already alarming growth of unemployment. In the end, both economic strategies have failed to address the basic needs of the Dominican people.

The great majority of Dominicans looking for jobs have been unable to find them in their home country. The growing lack of jobs has made it difficult for the common people to earn a living. Available figures show that many more women and men are looking for jobs of any kind than there are jobs available in the country. The wide disparity between willing workers and employment options becomes clear in the assessment put forward by the

**Table 2.3**
**Foreign Trade (In millions of $US)**

| Year | Exportation | Importation | Balance |
|------|-------------|-------------|---------|
| 1977 | 780 | 847 | −67 |
| 1978 | 676 | 860 | −184 |
| 1979 | 869 | 1,080 | −211 |
| 1980 | 962 | 1,498 | −536 |
| 1981 | 1,188 | 1,450 | −262 |
| 1982 | 768 | 1,248 | −480 |
| 1983 | 785 | 1,279 | −494 |
| 1984 | 868 | 1,257 | −389 |
| 1985 | 739 | 1,286 | −547 |
| 1986 | 722 | 1,266 | −544 |
| 1987 | 711 | 1,591 | −880 |
| 1988* | 890 | 1,600 | −710 |

*Preliminary

*Source:* Abreu et. al., 1989: 27. Used with permission.

Instituto de Población y Desarrollo, which calculated that, from 1980 to 1990, the Dominican labor force would increase by approximately 90,000 workers per year while the economy would produce only some 30,000 new jobs per year. These calculations assumed constancy in the birth and death rates as well as the same level of emigration, with zero return migration.

The comparison of the growth of the GNP and jobs shows that increasing unemployment is not related to a falling GNP, but rather to the incapacity of the forces of production to create enough jobs. From 1970 to 1981, the aggregated value of the agro-cattle sector increased from RD$345.2 million to 483.9 million, reflecting a growth of 40%, but the number of employed workers in the sector went up only 20%, from 502,634 to 602,908. During the same period, industrial production increased its aggregated value from RD$315.6 to 703.8, reflecting an extraordinary rise of 123%. Yet, the number of workers employed in the sector rose only 30%, from 113,040 to 147,086 (calculated from Santana and Tatis 1985:30).

It was clear by the end of the 1980s, then, that for many sectors of the working class, the country's economic growth did not translate into the creation of better jobs or new jobs. For the majority of the Dominican people, the behavior of the Dominican economy seemed irrelevant. No matter how well the economy performed, their economic conditions did not improve, and their fate remained uncertain. For instance, the 1968–1975 period is

**Table 2.4**
**Changes in the Distribution of Income in Santo Domingo from 1969 to 1973**

| Group of Income % of the Total Population | % of the Total Income of the Working Sectors | |
|---|---|---|
| | 1969 | 1973 |
| 20% (lowest) | 2.9 | 1.4 |
| 50% (low middle) | 17.6 | 15.4 |
| 30% (middle) | 27.6 | 30.2 |
| 20% (top) | 54.8 | 54.4 |

*Source:* Lozano 1985: 160. Used with permission.

identified by economists as the time of the greatest economic growth in Dominican history, but that period also witnessed increasing inequality, poverty, and social distress. A look at the changes in the distribution of income in Dominican society during the 1970s would show that the poor became poorer, but the other social strata largely benefited (see Table 2.4). Moreover, given the predominance of low wages in the restructured economy, even many employed workers found it impossible to fulfill their aspirations of social mobility.

From 1969 to 1973, the bottom fifth of the population, in the lowest income bracket, significantly reduced its share in the total income. This group experienced an extraordinary loss, declining from 2.9% in 1969 to 1.4% in 1973, reflecting a cut of almost a half of its earnings in four years. The top fifth of the population continued to hold its share, with 54.8% of the total income in 1969 and 54.4% in 1973, but the middle sector underwent a significant increase from 27.6% in 1969 to 30.2% in 1973 (Lozano 1985: 160). During Balaguer's first three presidential terms, the pattern of capitalist accumulation necessitated the development of an industrial, commercial, and financial bourgeoisie; the intense use of industrial sugar workers or peasant laborers; and the consolidation of an urban middle class. According to sociologist Wilfredo Lozano, the Dominican middle class can be divided into two subsectors on the basis of income and occupation. The lower middle class consists of an enlarged bureaucracy of low-wage workers, and the upper middle class comprises a reduced cadre of highly paid workers connected to the commercial and financial sectors. The latter subgroup became the primary clientele for imported goods and provided the main source of accumulation for the national bourgeoisie (Lozano 1985: 160–73).

## Table 2.5
## Poverty in the Dominican Republic (Millions of people and % of total population)

|             | 1984 | %    | 1989 | %    |
|-------------|------|------|------|------|
| Indigent    | 1.4  | 22.7 | 2.5  | 35.2 |
| Poor        | 1.5  | 24.0 | 1.5  | 20.8 |
| Total Poor  | 2.9  | 46.6 | 4.0  | 56.0 |

*Source:* Santana and Rathe 1993: 189–93. Used with permission.

Poverty in Dominican society has increased considerably during the last twenty years. A national survey conducted by the Central Bank between 1976 and 1977 found that 51.3% of the households in the country had a deficit in their monthly budget. These households earned 20.9% of the total income, but had a consumption of 26.0%. The same study showed that 90% of the population did not consume the recommended amount of nutrients and that 23.3% of the people fell below the poverty level (Del Rosario Mota and Madera Daniel 1984). By 1984, 40.8% of the children under five years of age were malnourished, and the number of families below the poverty level had doubled, rising to 47%, and increasing again to 56% by 1989 (Santana and Rathe 1993: 189). (See Table 2.5.)

Economists Isidoro Santana and Magdalena Rathe measured Dominican poverty using a methodology whereby the working population was classified according to household income and expenses and then divided into two groups. The poor were those below the poverty line and the nonpoor were above the line. Households where 60% or more of the income was spent on food were considered below the poverty line. Indigent households were those that, even after using all their income on food, could not attain an appropriate diet. They calculated that in 1989 the median poor (mid-income below the poverty line) needed to increase their income by 22% just to reach the classification of nonpoor. They thought it unlikely that the gap between the poor and nonpoor could be eliminated in the near future. They reasoned that "if the income of all the poor began a sustained increase of 3% per year, just the median poor would need 8 years to leave the category of poor, but those whose income fell below the mid-income poor, would remain so" (Santana and Rathe 1993: 89–91).

The 1980s were a difficult time for many Dominican workers. One could no longer speak of a landless peasantry, an industrial proletariat (whether linked to the sugar industries or the urban FTZ's), or workers in the informal economy. During the 1980s most workers who needed to work for a living

## Table 2.6
## Sectorial Evolution of Employed Population (Santo Domingo: 1980–1983)

|  | 1980 | 1983 | Rate of Growth |
|---|---|---|---|
| Government[1] | 24.6 | 22.2 | 2.5 |
| Modern Private[2] | 36.8 | 32.8 | 2.0 |
| Informal[3] | 26.7 | 32.5 | 14.8 |
| Domestic[4] | 11.4 | 11.6 | 7.3 |
| Other[5] | 0.5 | 0.9 | - |
| Total | 100 | 100 | 26.6 |

[1]Government Sector: Includes all persons employed in state institutions, including central government, independent, semi-independent, or state industries.

[2]Modern Private Sector: Includes all persons employed in industries, business, or private institutions with five workers or more. It also includes people with university education even if they work in places with fewer than five workers.

[3]Informal Sector: Includes those persons with education below the university level who work in private institutions and businesses with five workers or less. It excludes domestic service.

[4]Domestic Sector: Includes all persons who work by offering direct services in households other than their own.

[5]Other: Includes all persons not included in the above categories.

*Source:* Ceara Hatton, 1990a: 146. Used with permission.

suffered. The transference in benefit sustained by Balaguer's economic policies came to an end, particularly for the middle class. Middle-class sectors now realized that they were not exempt from peril. They lost jobs, and their salaries lost purchasing power. Stable and well-paid jobs were increasingly substituted by less desirable jobs. Between 1980 and 1983, for instance, the number of employed people in the modern private sector decreased from 36.8% to 32.8%, but the number of workers in the informal sector increased from 26.7% to 32.5% (see Table 2.6).

The median earnings in government jobs also went down from RD$251 to RD$233 (see Table 2.7). One could conclude that the precarious situation of Dominican workers was a result of the fall in the price of export products in the international market and an increase in the level of importation. Ultimately, though, the "crisis" has resulted from a structurally deformed economy bent on satisfying its increasing internal needs by importing, while producing mostly to comply with outside demands.

Balaguer's first twelve years of government came to an end in 1978. The Partido Revolucionario Dominicano (PRD) would rule for two terms from 1978 to 1986, to make way again for Balaguer, who would then remain in

**Table 2.7**
**Sectorial Median Income (RD$ monthly, 1980–1983)**

|  | 1980 | 1983 | Difference |
|---|---|---|---|
| Government | 251 | 233 | −7.0 |
| Modern | 308 | 300 | −1.6 |
| Informal | 195 | 181 | −4.0 |
| Domestic | 58 | 55 | −5.2 |

*Source:* Adapted from Ceara Hatton 1990a: 184. Used with permission.

**Table 2.8**
**Investment and Jobs in Agribusiness (in RD$)**

|  | 1983 | 1984 | 1985 |
|---|---|---|---|
| Total Investment | 112,031,707 | 49,676,234 | 156,793,476 |
| Total Jobs Created | 2,508 | 2,365 | 2,990 |
| Agricultural Jobs | (1,885) | (1,453) | (1,555) |
| Industrial Jobs | (623) | (912) | (1,435) |

*Source:* Adapted from Moya Pons 1992: 387. Used with permission.

office until August 1996. The first PRD government, headed by President Antonio Guzmán, followed the Keynesian model of direct government intervention by increasing the level of investment to stimulate economic activity and generate jobs. Guzmán's term in office witnessed the expansion of the aggregate demand through the infusion of state funds, an increase in real salaries, and the growth of cattle-agriculture production (Ceara Hatton and Croes Hernández 1993: 14). Unemployment remained high, though. The new jobs created, particularly in the public sector and the agribusiness industries (see Tables 2.8 and 2.9), did not suffice to absorb the inactive workforce. Similarly, the jobs created in the public sector were nonproductive in nature, and the agribusiness industries centered around activities requiring advanced technology and specialized skills, disproportionately limiting the number of workers needed in relation to the amount of capital invested.

**Table 2.9**
**Dominican Republic Public Sector Workers from 1950 to 1986**

| Year | Total | Year | Total |
|------|-------|------|-------|
| 1950 | 40,476 | 1972 | 97,413 |
| 1951 | 47,703 | 1973 | 100,184 |
| 1952 | 50,391 | 1974 | 111,899 |
| 1953 | 46,429 | 1975 | 116,946 |
| 1954 | 46,292 | 1976 | 119,423 |
| 1955 | 55,390 | 1977 | 122,341 |
| 1956 | 61,692 | 1978 | 123,018 |
| 1957 | 71,269 | 1979 | 144,090 |
| 1958 | 77,926 | 1980 | 170,216 |
| 1959 | 81,546 | 1981 | 195,411 |
| 1960 | 84,934 | 1982 | 211,595 |
| 1961 | 88,026 | 1983 | 227,247 |
| 1962 | 110,349 | 1984 | 210,133 |
| 1963 | 112,568 | 1985 | 220,574 |
| 1964 | 112,002 | 1986 | 219,690 |
| 1965 | 99,159 | | |
| 1966 | 97,999 | | |
| 1967 | 98,728 | | |
| 1968 | 96,584 | | |
| 1969 | 93,281 | | |
| 1970 | 98,899 | | |
| 1971 | 100,230 | | |

*Source:* Gómez and Báez 1988: 25. Used with permission.

### THE GREAT ESCAPE

As the economy continued to deteriorate in the 1980s, there developed a new feature in Dominican migration: a sharp increase in the number of professional and technical workers who emigrated because of the decline of public services, the drastic fall in the value of the Dominican peso, and the loss of stable and well-paid jobs in the sending society. By 1991 the purchasing power of the minimum wage reflected half the value it had had in the 1970s. Salary readjustment in the large companies of the modern sector brought these salaries down to 60% of their value in the 1970s. During the 1980s, members of the middle-class sectors did not escape the negative effects of the economic changes occurring in the country. One could argue that the expatriation of surplus laborers during the 1970s, and the direct transferring of resources from the poor and less privileged sectors, favored the middle class. But the economic restructuring of the 1980s provoked a widespread displacement that engulfed portions of the middle class, whose members felt the need to seek the same solution regularly sought by the less privileged groups: emigration.

The exodus from the Dominican Republic to the United States accelerated. The number of Dominicans leaving home increased at an incredible speed. Among those who are still leaving the country for the United States, the unskilled members of the working class continue to represent the overwhelming majority. They are mostly dark-skinned, and in their ranks women outnumber men. Ironically, Dominicans come to a receiving society which has for some time been undergoing its own economic restructuring. The kinds of jobs they, as new immigrants, will most likely qualify for have been gradually disappearing. They have come into a racially stratified society where blacks and other dark people suffer marginalization. At the time when Dominicans first began to arrive in the United States, Puerto Ricans had already been living here for decades without achieving significant economic progress as a group. A team of social scientists who studied Puerto Rican migrants during the 1960s described the scenario awaiting the newcomers as follows:

Many of the [Puerto Rican] migrants are women, in a society where women's economic lot is still often difficult; many are Negroes, in a society in which color counts heavily against them; and most of the migrants—both Negroes and whites, both women and men—are without much skill, in a society where skill is increasingly important to adequate livelihood; and all enter a society where the opportunities for advancement seem increasingly to narrow for the poor, the uneducated, and the "foreign." (Mills, Senior, and Goldsen 1950: 38–39)

The irony is that the lugubrious scenario associated with Puerto Ricans decades earlier accords fittingly with the situation encountered by Dominican immigrants on their arrival in the receiving society. What remains to be seen is whether the changes being proposed in the United States to curtail immigration, particularly of blue-collar and unskilled workers, will leave the Dominican power structure without an open door to the United States through which diligently and quietly to expel surplus labor, and whether the Dominicans already living in the United States can survive as a group in a milieu that has become unfriendly toward the immigrant.

# 3

# *Dominicans in the United States: The Rise of a Community*

## LABOR MARKET EXPERIENCE

Huge numbers of Dominicans have moved out of their home country in search of a better life in North America. According to the U.S. Census, in 1990 511,297 Dominicans were living as permanent residents in the United States; over 65% of them were residing in the state of New York. The rest of the Dominican population in the United States is spread throughout the country, with the most numerous contingents residing—in descending order—in the following states: New Jersey, Florida, Massachusetts, Rhode Island, Connecticut, California, Maryland, Texas, Pennsylvania, and Washington.

The labor market experience of immigrants in the receiving society is commonly used as a reliable measure of their levels of prosperity. Their job market, earnings, rates of labor force participation, and patterns of employment are among the salient indicators used to measure progress. At the same time, each one of these variables is affected by the type of workers the productive market needs and the value ascribed to the immigrant workers' abilities and skills. If the abilities and skills of an immigrant group are badly needed and highly valued in the receiving society, that group will most likely have high rates of employment and competitive earnings. The plight of the same immigrant group, however, will differ notably if its abilities and skills abound in the receiving society. Ultimately, the material well-being of immigrants will be determined not only by their incorporation into the labor market of the host country but also by the nature of that incorporation.

Three Dominican *comadres* outside a schoolyard in Manhattan. © Josefina Báez.

## Table 3.1
## Dominican Population of New York City, by Borough

| New York City Borough | Number | | Percentage of Total Dominican Pop., 1990 |
|---|---|---|---|
| | 1980 | 1990 | |
| Manhattan | 62,660 | 136,696 | 41.1% |
| The Bronx | 17,640 | 87,261 | 26.2 |
| Brooklyn | 21,140 | 55,301 | 16.6 |
| Queens | 23,780 | 52,309 | 15.7 |
| Staten Island | 160 | 1,146 | 0.4 |
| Total | 125,380 | 332,713 | 100.0 |

*Source:* Hernández, Rivera-Batiz, and Agodini 1995: 7. Used with permission.

As explained in the Preface, we will concentrate on Dominicans in New York City to illustrate the Dominican-American experience.

The 1990 U.S. Census showed that New York City alone accounted for over 93% of those Dominicans who had come to New York State. From 1980 to 1990, the Dominican population of the city which increased from 125,380 to 332,713, showed the largest growth of any ethnic group in the city for that period (see Table 3.1). This remarkable numerical gain was the result of a constant and growing immigration influx (see Figure 2.1). Their massive arrival occurred, however, at a time when New York City was undergoing a socioeconomic restructuring that would have a remarkable impact on the need for and value of labor as well as on the creation of jobs. The socioeconomic restructuring of New York City has been well studied by other scholars. Our concern with it here is limited to those details that may help shed light on the position of Dominicans in the labor market.

The city has undergone a clear economic transformation in as much as activities of the service sector have come to replace an economy formerly based predominantly on industrial production. As a result of this change, New York has often been described as a postindustrial city. Scholars trace to the 1950s the beginning of the process whereby the large manufacturing sector, which had characterized the economic life of the city, suffered a gradual decline. We have now seen the shrinking of that sector manifested in the disappearance of hundreds of thousands of manufacturing jobs, particularly in the garment industry, the largest area of industrial production. From 1969 to 1985, for instance, the city lost 465,000 manufacturing jobs (Drennan 1991: 29). The restructuring process dislocated not only the productive jobs directly but also a wide variety of other jobs that were tangentially connected to manufacturing. Entire industrial headquarters moved out, and with them went a host of employment opportunities. In a period of twenty years (1969 to 1989), wholesale trade jobs declined from 309,000 to 229,000, and trucking and warehousing positions went down from 41,000 to 26,000 (Drennan 1991: 32). Overall, the decline in employment occurred primarily among blue-collar and unskilled workers who suffered from 1970 to 1986 the loss of 510,000 jobs in fields that required less than twelve years of education (Kasarda 1990: 247).

## PRIOR TO MIGRATION

The labor market experience of Dominicans prior to migration matters to the extent that it will influence their integration into the job market of the receiving society. During the 1970s, one out of every four Dominicans migrating to the United States was a blue-collar worker, specifically an operative, and three in every fifty had had a professional or technical career. Also, fewer than one out of every two was likely to have had an occupation at the time of migrating to the United States.[1] During the 1980s, the pattern changed slightly since many more Dominicans, particularly males, reported to have had an occupation before departure. Although blue-collar workers continued to predominate in the migratory flow by a very large margin, during that decade the number of professional and technical workers migrating exceeded that of the 1970s. The data reflect that during the 1980s more than one out of every two Dominican males was likely to have had an occupation before migration, and less than one out of every two women was likely to have had one. Similarly, out of every twenty-five males, two were likely to have had a professional or technical skill, and approximately nine were likely to have worked as operatives. Out of every fourteen women admitted, one reported to have a professional or technical career, and one out of every eight identified herself as an operative worker, according to the Department of City Planning's *The Newest New Yorkers: An Analysis of Immigration into New York City During the 1980s* (1992). The data included only Dominicans who were between sixteen and sixty-four years old, and those who did not report an occupation were subdivided into students, unemployed, and homemakers.

## DISTRIBUTION OF DOMINICAN WORKERS

The industrial distribution for the 1980s and 1990s of a few prominent ethnic groups compared in New York City[2] would suggest that in both

**Table 3.2**
**Industrial Distribution of the Labor Force in New York City**
**from 1979 to 1989 (Persons 16 years of age or older)**

| Industry | Non-Hispanic White | Non-Hispanic Black | Hispanic | Dominican |
|---|---|---|---|---|
| Agriculture and Forestry | 0.5 | 0.3 | 0.5 | 0.3 |
| Mining and Construction | 4.9 | 4.2 | 4.9 | 4.3 |
| Manufacturing | 10.9 | 8.2 | 18.6 | 25.7 |
| Transportation, Communications, and Public Utility (TCPU) | 8.2 | 11.7 | 7.6 | 6.6 |
| Trade | 17.9 | 14.2 | 22.5 | 27.6 |
| Finance, Insurance, and Real Estate (FIRE) | 13.1 | 10.1 | 8.6 | 5.5 |
| Professional Services (Health, Educat.) | 28.7 | 32.0 | 19.7 | 14.4 |
| Business Services | 6.2 | 7.1 | 7.0 | 6.8 |
| Personal/Entertainment Services | 5.5 | 5.8 | 7.0 | 7.0 |
| Public Administration | 4.1 | 6.5 | 3.6 | 1.9 |

*Source:* Hernández, Rivera-Batiz, and Agodini 1995:43. Used with permission.

decades Dominicans held by far the highest percentage of jobs in manufacturing (see Table 3.2). In 1990, 25.7 percent of Dominicans sixteen years of age or older worked in that sector. During the same year, the percentages for Hispanics, including Puerto Ricans, was 18.6; for non-Hispanic whites, 10.9; and for non-Hispanic blacks, 8.2. Compared to 1980, in 1990 Dominicans reduced their participation in the manufacturing industry considerably. The reduction, connected to the overall shift that started in the 1950s and has led to a transformed economy, may be said to have had a disproportionate impact on Dominican workers, who lost nearly half of the positions they had held in that sector, reducing their labor force participation from 48.6% to 25.7%.

The drastic loss of manufacturing jobs among Dominicans stemmed from a sectorial decline and the market's inability to retrieve workers after its transformation. Since the 1950s, the manufacturing sector has narrowed its employment potential. The industry's creation of new jobs has not altered the tendency to hire ever fewer workers. Manufacturing underwent changes that diminished the need for labor. Thousands of small firms emerged throughout New York City and Long Island that did not offer standardized products to a general public. These small, customer-oriented firms cater to the needs of small clienteles. These new firms, ranging from electronics (particularly for the defense industry) to apparel and furniture, employ only a small fraction of the total labor force of the city (O'Neill and Moss 1991: 10).

Many of the new industries do not require a large workforce for production. Generally, they produce for a small and selected clientele whose primary requirement is quality, not quantity. Moreover, their production is organized around "intellectual capital," meaning the combination of "patents, processes, management skills, technologies, information about customers and suppliers, and old-fashioned experience," as defined by Hugh O'Neill and Mitchell L. Moss (1991: 9). That is to say that, although these industries could draw from an intensive use of labor rather than of capital, their level of output is reduced in scale. Their production remains linked to an overall labor force that cannot be completely unskilled. The apparel industry, for instance, the largest area of production within manufacturing, is the one that absorbs the largest number of Dominican workers. However, that sector did not expand its number of jobs although it did respond to local demand by transforming into small shops oriented to the production of elaborate and expensive clothing for exclusive customers. From 1984 to 1987, the apparel industry lost 12.5 percent of its share in the labor market without compensating for the job loss during the period (Department of City Planning 1991: 44). In the 1980s Dominicans began to move to the service sector, as evinced by their increasing participation in trade and professional services (see Table 3.2). Compared to the other ethnic groups, Dominicans had the highest percentage of people employed in trade in 1990. Employment in trade for Dominicans represented 27.6 percent, as compared with 17.9 percent for non-Hispanic whites, 14.1 percent for non-Hispanic blacks, and 22.5 percent for Hispanics in general. The area of trade in which Dominicans most often find employment tends to deal with retail, particularly restaurants, bars, bodegas, and apparel, shoe, and accessory stores.

The movement of Dominicans to the service sector has in no way compensated their loss of jobs in the manufacturing industry. On the contrary, it has entailed increased unemployment along with reduced labor force participation rates. In practice it would seem that they are facing expulsion from a declining job market with only a moderate insertion into the less spacious areas of another job market, that is, into areas characterized by a slow or negative growth. Although Dominicans have increased their participation rate in the service sector, their participation not only is quantitatively limited, but also occurs in the least dynamic sections of that sector. Substantial growth in the service sector has occurred within the FIRE industries (finance, insurance, real estate) as well as in government jobs but not in trade or the TCPU industries (transportation, communication, and public utilities), which are service sector job markets where the participation of Dominicans has moderately increased (see Figure 3.1). Trade and TCPU in general suffered an absolute job loss in the 1980s. Compared to the other ethnic groups, Dominicans had the lowest representation in the FIRE industries as well as in public administration jobs in 1990 (see Table 3.3).

## OCCUPATIONS AND EARNINGS

The current occupational distribution among Dominicans, according to the 1990 census, indicates that they are highly underrepresented in the professional and managerial categories. Only 9.6 percent of Dominicans were employed in professional and managerial jobs in 1990, compared to non-Hispanic whites, 38.5 percent; non-Hispanic blacks, 19.6 percent; and Hispanics, 13.9 percent (Table 3.3). Dominican workers also hold the highest proportion of blue-collar and unskilled jobs (laborers and operators), clearly showing an overrepresentation in that occupational rank.

Nevertheless, although in 1990 Dominicans continued to be overrepresented in blue-collar manufacturing jobs, itself an area of employment characterized by precariousness, the figures show that during the 1980s they lost a solid 15.9% share in that job market too (Table 3.4). Other than their modest increase of 7.3% in middle and low white-collar jobs (technical, sales, and clerical) from 1980 to 1990, they did not obtain significant gains in the higher occupational categories of the service sector. In short, their loss of shares in manufacturing, combined with their modest gain in the service sector during the 1980s, would paint an unfavorable picture of the condition of Dominicans in the U.S. labor market, assuming that New York City can adequately serve as a useful ground for making that assessment.

Data on the distribution of earnings show that, in 1990, compared to the other ethnic groups, Dominicans did badly. Similarly, during the 1980s, the earning gap between Dominicans and the highest earners (non-Hispanic

**Figure 3.1**
**New York City Industry Distribution**

### 1960

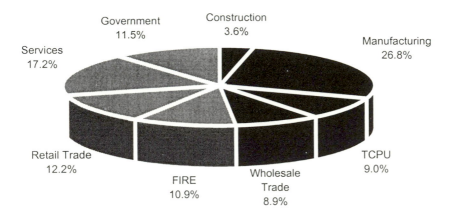

Government
11.5%

Construction
3.6%

Manufacturing
26.8%

Services
17.2%

Retail Trade
12.2%

FIRE
10.9%

Wholesale
Trade
8.9%

TCPU
9.0%

### 1990

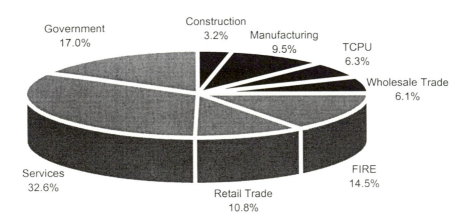

Government
17.0%

Construction
3.2%

Manufacturing
9.5%

TCPU
6.3%

Wholesale Trade
6.1%

Services
32.6%

Retail Trade
10.8%

FIRE
14.5%

Industrial Sector

Services Sector

*Source:* Department of City Planning 1993: 4.

**Table 3.3**
**Occupational Distribution of the Labor Force in New York City:**
**Four Groups (Persons 16 years of age or older)**

| Occupation | Non-Hispanic White (%) | Non-Hispanic Black (%) | Hispanic (%) | Dominican (%) |
|---|---|---|---|---|
| Managerial and Professional | 38.5 | 19.6 | 13.9 | 9.6 |
| Technical, Sales, and Administrative Support | 35.6 | 36.6 | 30.9 | 27.1 |
| Service Workers | 10.1 | 24.0 | 23.1 | 22.5 |
| Farming, Forestry, and Fishing | 0.4 | 0.4 | 0.6 | 0.4 |
| Precision Product, Craft, and Repair | 7.8 | 6.6 | 9.4 | 9.6 |
| Operators, Fabricators, and Laborers | 7.6 | 12.8 | 22.1 | 30.9 |

*Source:* Hernández, Rivera-Batiz, and Agodini 1995: 37. Used with permission.

whites) became wider. After one adjusts for inflation, the average annual salary of Dominican males in 1989 was $15,139; non-Hispanic whites earned $36,272; non-Hispanic blacks, $20,707; and Hispanics, $18,540. In 1989 the annual wage of Dominican males increased modestly, but the gap between them and non-Hispanic white male workers widened considerably (see Table 3.5). In 1979, in other words, for every dollar earned by non-Hispanic white males, Dominican males earned only 48.7 cents, which went down to 41.7 cents in 1989. In 1979 the average Dominican male earned 78 cents per every dollar earned by the average Hispanic male. In 1989 the gap closed slightly when the earning of Dominican males increased by 3 cents. The reduction of that gap, however, did not correspond to a betterment for Dominican males. Rather, the annual earnings of Hispanic males, compared to the rest of the other male workers, experienced the lowest increase—3.5 percent between 1979 and 1989. Dominican women, on their part, also exhibit lower wages when compared to other women in the city. In 1989 the average annual earnings for a Dominican woman was $11,371, compared to a non-Hispanic white woman who, on the average, earned $23,521; a non-Hispanic black woman, $18,695; and a Hispanic woman, $14,553.

**Table 3.4**
**Occupational Distribution of the Labor Force in New York City:**
**Two Groups (Persons 16 years of age and older)**

| Occupation | Overall New York City | | Dominican | |
|---|---|---|---|---|
| | 1980 | 1990 | 1980 | 1990 |
| Managerial and Professional | 24.7% | 28.8% | 4.7% | 9.6% |
| Technical, Sales, and Administrative Support | 36.3 | 34.9 | 19.8 | 27.1 |
| Service Workers | 15.2 | 16.2 | 18.7 | 22.5 |
| Farming, Forestry, and Fishing | 0.5 | 0.4 | 0.3 | 0.4 |
| Precision Product, Craft, and Repair | 8.3 | 7.7 | 9.3 | 9.6 |
| Operators, Fabricators, and Laborers | 15.0 | 12.1 | 46.8 | 30.9 |

*Source:* Hernández, Rivera-Batiz, and Agodini 1995: 38. Used with permission.

Their wage in that year increased from $10,007 to $11,371, a much too modest change when compared with non-Hispanic white women whose average salary went from $17,411 to $23,521 (Table 3.5). In 1979 a Dominican woman earned 57.4 cents per every dollar earned by a non-Hispanic white woman, and this gap had widened by 1989 when her earnings fell to 48.3 cents with respect to her white counterpart.

## EMPLOYMENT, UNEMPLOYMENT, OUTCOMES

Dominican men in 1990 had a labor force participation of 73.1 percent, the highest rate in relation to the other ethnic groups. Dominican women had an almost similar degree of involvement in the labor market when compared with other Hispanic women; 49.1 percent and 49.2 percent, respectively.

Overall, during the 1980s, the labor force participation rates of Dominican men and women were negatively affected (see Table 3.6). Among the other ethnic groups, in 1990 Dominican males were the only ones who experienced a decline of 2.5 percent in their participation rate in the labor force. Com-

**Table 3.5**
**Changes in Annual Earnings in New York City from 1979 to 1989 (Employed persons 16 years of age or older)**

| Population Group | 1979 Earnings (1989$) | 1989 Earnings | % Change (1980–1990) |
|---|---|---|---|
| **MEN** | | | |
| Dominican | 13,982 | 15,139 | 8.3 |
| New York City overall | 25,141 | 28,815 | 14.6 |
| Non-Hispanic white | 28,653 | 36,272 | 26.6 |
| Non-Hispanic black | 19,410 | 20,703 | 8.2 |
| Hispanic overall | 17,908 | 18,540 | 3.5 |
| **WOMEN** | | | |
| Dominican | 10,007 | 11,371 | 13.6 |
| New York City overall | 16,304 | 20,425 | 25.3 |
| Non-Hispanic white | 17,411 | 23,521 | 35.1 |
| Non-Hispanic black | 15,566 | 18,695 | 20.1 |
| Hispanic overall | 12,611 | 14,553 | 15.4 |

*Source:* Hernández, Rivera-Batiz, and Agodini 1995: 31. Used with permission.

pared to 1980, Dominican women experienced a slight increase of 1.8 percent, but their increase lagged substantially behind those of the women in the other ethnic groups, who experienced increases ranging from 5.8 percent to 8.3. In 1980 Dominican women had a higher labor force participation rate (47.3%) than Hispanic women in general (41.2%), but in 1990 the gap was closed and surpassed by Hispanic women who moved to 49.2 percent. Similarly, while in 1980 Dominican women almost equaled the labor force participation rates of women overall in the city (47.3 percent for Dominicans and 47.8 percent for women overall in New York City), in 1990 they fell behind by 5.5 percent. At the same time, from 1980 to 1990, unemployment went up among Dominican women from 9.5 percent to 18.4 percent; among other women it increased only 1 percent for non-Hispanic black women and 1.5 percent for other New York women.

**Table 3.6**
**Labor Force Participation Rates, New York City, from 1980 to 1990 (Persons 16 years of age or older)**

| | Labor Force Participation Rate (%) | | | |
| | Male | | Female | |
| Population Group | 1980 | 1990 | 1980 | 1990 |
|---|---|---|---|---|
| Dominican | 75.6 | 73.1 | 47.3 | 49.1 |
| New York City overall | 70.5 | 71.8 | 47.8 | 54.6 |
| Non-Hispanic white | 71.8 | 72.4 | 47.5 | 53.3 |
| Non-Hispanic black | 65.0 | 67.8 | 51.9 | 60.2 |
| Hispanic overall | 70.6 | 72.6 | 41.2 | 49.2 |

*Source:* Hernández, Rivera-Batiz, and Agodini 1995: 27. Used with permission.

## EDUCATION AND RESIDENTIAL PATTERNS

The foregoing discussion could partially explain poor labor market outcomes among Dominican workers. There is evidence that Dominicans have a low educational attainment, a high proportion of blue-collar and unskilled workers, and a limited English proficiency. They also tend to reside almost exclusively in urban areas. Their underrepresentation in upper white-collar occupations accords with their low educational attainment. Similarly, their limited English proficiency (LEP) affects their likelihood to move to middle and low white-collar jobs as well as to the public sector. In 1990 Dominicans had the highest proportion of persons twenty-five years of age or older who had not completed high school (see Table 3.7); 52.3 percent of Dominicans twenty-five years of age or older had completed less than high school. Among the groups compared, Dominicans also had the smallest representation among people twenty-five years of age or older who had completed college or more. Only 8 percent of Dominicans had completed college or more, compared to 29.9 percent of the overall population of the city, 41.6 percent of non-Hispanic whites, 15.6 percent of non-Hispanic blacks, and 10.9 percent of Hispanics. In 1980, 72 percent of Dominicans twenty-five years of age or older had less than a high school education; in 1990, this total went down to 52.2 percent.

Arguably, residential patterns may have also affected labor market outcomes among Dominican workers. As indicated previously, most Domini-

**Table 3.7**
**Educational Status of the Population in New York City, 1990**
**(Persons 25 years of age or older)**

| Population Group | Percentage of the Population Completing | | | |
|---|---|---|---|---|
| | Less than High School | High School | Some College | College or More |
| Dominican | 52.3 | 20.4 | 19.3 | 8.0 |
| New York City overall | 20.8 | 24.8 | 24.5 | 29.9 |
| Non-Hispanic white | 11.7 | 23.2 | 23.5 | 41.6 |
| Non-Hispanic black | 24.9 | 29.9 | 29.6 | 15.6 |
| Hispanic | 40.4 | 25.6 | 23.1 | 10.9 |

*Source:* Hernández, Rivera-Batiz, and Agodini 1995: 34. Used with permission.

cans admitted to the United States live in New York City. Though their percentage in New York City has steadily declined since the 1970s, due to their progressive spreading out to other neighboring cities, 65.1 percent of all Dominicans in the United States in 1990 claimed this city as their home. This matters because job growth, particularly blue-collar and low-skilled service jobs, was highest in the suburbs and their intermediate and outer areas, which are distant from Dominican settlements. "Between 1978 and 1989, for example, employment in grocery retailing in New York and New Jersey suburbs increased by 25 percent. But in New York's outer boroughs it increased by less than 1 percent" (O'Neill and Moss 1991: 57). Similarly, while wholesale employment in Manhattan, for instance, experienced an absolute loss of 27,300 jobs, the outer-ring suburbs had an absolute gain of 28,100 wholesale jobs (1991: 52). The fact that over 20 percent of Dominican homes did not own a telephone in 1990 and the high cost of public transportation to and from these regions must have contributed to the isolation of Dominicans.

The shifting of the economy from manufacturing to service and the increasing loss of good paying blue-collar, unskilled jobs had a devastating effect on Dominican workers who, on the basis of their prior training or lack thereof, depended on those jobs. During the 1980s, for instance, the Dominican Republic outnumbered all other Caribbean nations in the proportion of unskilled, blue-collar workers it sent to New York City. From 1982 to 1989, 36.6 percent of Dominican arrivals were specifically classified as operators and laborers. The corresponding proportion for the entire Caribbean region, excluding the Dominican Republic, was 21.4 percent, as may be gathered from figures provided by the Department of City Planning (1992: 69–70).

Labor force participation rate among Dominicans was relatively high during the 1970s due perhaps to the volume of their migration and the momentary need for workers caused by the socioeconomic changes taking place in the manufacturing sector. There was considerable variation in the mean annual admission of immigrants from the Dominican Republic from 1966 to 1985: 12,579 in the first decade (1966 to 1975) and 18,316 in the second (1976 to 1985). Their increasing and constant migration, combined with the arrival of other groups who were attracted to the same employment options, has probably saturated their natural job markets, which have become ever narrower in light of the city's economic transformation. In short, Dominican immigrants currently confront serious socioeconomic challenges as a result of the restructured economy of the receiving society.

## DOMINICANS IN BUSINESS

Despite the precariousness of their community's socioeconomic profile, Dominicans have established their presence in the realm of commercial activity. Predominantly Dominican neighborhoods visibly display active commercial areas made up of retail business that provide services and goods primarily for community residents. In Washington Heights/Inwood, stores owned or operated by Dominicans stand out as one of the most significant economic phenomena in the area. Distinctively Dominican signs and symbols, such as the Dominican flag, revered historical figures, names of battles, provinces, and towns, adorn the myriad storefronts along Broadway, Saint Nicholas, Audubon, and Amsterdam avenues in northern Manhattan.

Academic observers of Dominican migration have invariably highlighted the emergence of this community as an important business constituency. They have celebrated the entrepreneurial spirit of Dominican immigrants, whom they describe as a shrewd people who created business alternatives from grocery stores to garment production in order to escape unemployment or dead-end low-paying jobs in the secondary labor market. In describing her impressions of Dominicans in Washington Heights, Linda Chavez, author of *Out of the Barrio*, notes, "The vibrant commercial areas, even the

Dominican youngsters playing outside. © Josefina Báez.

manner in which the people moved on the street attested to the vitality of the neighborhood" (Chavez 1990: 152). Similarly, a New York journalist recorded her favorable impression of the number of businesses in Washington Heights presumably owned by Dominicans. She hailed their economic success among immigrants, in an article whose celebratory tone rings clear in the title: "For Dominican Immigrants the American Dream Lives On" (Junco 1997: 4).

Most Dominican entrepreneurs learn their business skills on the job while employed in ethnic economic enclaves. An ethnic economic enclave, as defined by Alejandro Portes and Robert Bach in a study of Cubans and Mexicans in the United States (1985), is a conglomerate of firms of any size owned and managed by members of a differentiated cultural or national minority. Often, start-up capital for opening a small business is generated by Dominican money lenders who do not require from borrowers any legal or formal documentation as a guarantee for the money lent. Capital may also be obtained from relatives and friends who may be interested in getting into business and want to invest their savings. It is generally believed that the business sector becomes a source of employment for compatriots and other members of ethnic minority groups, which compensates to a large extent for the dead-end and low-paid jobs in the secondary labor market.

Worthy of note is the role of Dominicans in the recent rise of independent supermarkets catering to inner-city retailing in New York, New Jersey, and Connecticut. The leadership of the National Supermarkets Association (NSA), whose president in 1995, Pablo Espinal, declared a membership of 400 independent supermarket owners, is Dominican. Such stores as C-Town, Bravo, Associated, Super Food, Pioneer, Compare Food, Fine Fare, and Clarimar, among others, are affiliates of the NSA. In an article inserted in a magazine published on the occasion of their Gala Banquet on November 11, 1995, NSA Vice President Mariano Díaz offered some useful background to the organization. He explained that entrepreneurs like him and the other NSA members rushed to fill the void created by the flight of the national chains decades ago from the ghettos of urban America. He credits independent food wholesalers, particularly his own supplier Krasdale Foods, with providing the vital start-up economic support that has made possible the success of many NSA members. In his words, "This is the most remarkable example of a large corporation encouraging entrepreneurship" (Díaz 1995: pages unnumbered). Díaz claims that the NSA has contributed to revitalizing such New York City areas as Harlem, the South Bronx, East New York, and Williamsburg, which had turned into symbols of urban decay. "We have," he contends, "along with the Korean green grocers, re-invented inner city retailing. We have revitalized hundreds of rundown commercial strips. . . . In the process, we have created thousands of jobs for community residents" (Díaz 1995).

Most Dominican economic ventures cluster around the service and the manufacturing sectors. The service area could be divided into three categories: (1) commercial activities that range from those involving food vendors (grocers, supermarket owners, ethnic restaurateurs) to those managing department stores (clothing, shoes, household appliances, and so on); (2) personal and business services (beauty parlors, insurance agencies, car service, travel agencies, and professional legal services); and (3) finance firms (one bank and a variety of money transfer agencies). Beside their diversity, some activities in the service sector reflect a high level of market share. An ethnographic study among Dominican business owners found that approximately 70% of all *bodegas* (grocery stores) in New York City, with estimated annual sales of $1.8 billion, were owned by Dominicans (Portes and Guarnizo 1991: 11).

Manufacturing ventures among Dominicans began early in the 1970s; service sector activities developed a decade later. The difference in timing has to do with the type of clientele to whom the economic activities are oriented. Contrary to manufacturing, service ventures require the formation of a large pool of effective consumers. The large and constant influx of Dominicans in the 1970s and thereafter led to the formation of a mass of customers whose patterns of consumption gave rise to the development of several small-scale enterprises catering to the growing community. Dominican ventures into manufacturing occurred differently. Garment production among Dominicans emerged as subcontracting factories, which are centers working for large manufacturing firms that are inserted in the larger economy and consumer spectrum. As such, most manufacturing firms are located outside the limits of Dominican neighborhoods. An ethnographic study on ownership among Dominicans in Washington Heights found that the average age of a manufacturing firm was 17.4 years; service sector firms had an average age of 5.8 years in business (Guarnizo 1993: 205). The same study established that manufacturing firms tend to have an average of 27 workers; service sector firms employ an average of 20.5 workers (1993: 257).

On the whole, ethnographic research among Dominican entrepreneurs has led to one of two contending views. Some analysts perceive Dominican business practically as a survival strategy. In other words, a Dominican business sector has developed in response to unemployment as well as dead-end low-paying jobs, but the sector does not represent more than a mechanism of survival for a thriving proletariat (Waldinger 1986: 166). Other analysts perceive the business sectors among Dominicans as an impressive economic enclave, resembling the early stage of Cuban capitalism in Miami. The proponents of this view argue that the immigrant enclave economy in question replicates itself in the home country (Portes and Guarnizo 1991). The theory of the enclave is based on the diversity and the size of the Dominican entrepreneur sector.

## WHO ARE THE BUSINESS OWNERS?

Dominican businesses are disproportionally owned by men. Luis Guarnizo, who has studied Dominican-owned firms in New York and the Dominican Republic, found that for every five owners only one was a woman (Guarnizo 1993). The average owner is a Dominican-born middle-aged, married man. Businesswomen are largely underrepresented in manufacturing; most of them own small service sector firms, such as beauty parlors and food-vending operations. These activities require low-scale start-up investment, which makes them highly susceptible to competition. Most women involved in manufacturing own small production centers often located in their own homes. These operations, generally informal and involving primarily sewing jobs, have on the average from one (the owner herself) to five workers who are paid on a piecework basis. They tend to be subcontracted to larger

Dominican-owned factories located in the city's garment district. The first major study that examined Dominican businesses in the garment industry found that, on the average, Dominican owners came from a rural background and had attained 9.9 years of schooling (Waldinger 1986: 176). However, Guarnizo subsequently observed that "the Dominican entrepreneurs interviewed possess impressive levels of formal schooling. A full third had finished college or graduate studies" (Guarnizo 1993: 121–22). Many Dominican immigrants who go into business are professionals (medical doctors, dentists, engineers, and lawyers) who have had to go outside of their areas of expertise to pursue their economic goals.

## ASSESSING THE BUSINESS SECTOR

The restructuring of the city in the last three decades created the conditions for Dominican entrepreneurship as it currently exists. Structural changes in manufacturing created opportunities for immigrant capitalists. From the 1920s to the 1950s, New York City teemed with manufacturers, housing the largest garment production in the nation. Yet, in the years that followed, three interconnected events would change the nature of this industry. First, during the 1950s, seeking to reduce the cost of labor which was high by international standards due to successful labor organizing, manufacturing firms began to leave the city in search for more profitable conditions. Second, Jews and Italians, who had controlled most manufacturing production in the city, began to step out of the business. Their children, having already acquired the appropriate tools to enter white-collar positions, did not choose to follow in the footsteps of their parents. And third, garment production itself changed considerably, leaning toward the creation of nonstandardized, fashionable merchandise. As a result of these changes, garment production tended to rely heavily on a large contingent of cheap workers, reducing the need for sophisticated technology. These factors, combined with an increased availability of factory space, which depressed the cost of rent, made it economically affordable for less affluent immigrants to venture into manufacturing (Waldinger 1986).

While structural causes changed the nature of garment production, demographic changes occurring after 1965 altered the ethnic balance of the city, creating in the process new pools of people with specific needs and interests. In effect, the increased influx of immigrants, particularly from the Third World, drastically affected the ethnic composition of the city and generated an abundant supply of cheap laborers, who were eager and ready to work and whose needs had to be met. The tendency of immigrants to settle in communities formed by people sharing their cultural background led to the formation of certain ethnically differentiated districts. Their high concentration in often overcrowded neighborhoods; their "foreign" tastes, which existing companies were unprepared to cater to; their need for basic personal services; and their desire to deal with their own people in their own language all stimulated the emergence of ethnic-specific enterprises. The continuous flow of immigrants into the city also allowed immigrant capitalists to draw from an abundant pool of cheap workers, of their own ethnic background, to fuel their bourgeoning economic activities. The combination of an abundant supply of cheap labor, the reduced cost of opening a business, and the readiness of the immigrant communities themselves to support the efforts of their own people largely explains the visibility of Dominicans in the business sector.

Many academic observers see Dominicans prospering as a result of their presence in the business sector. However, the 1990 U.S. Census reported that only 7% of Dominicans residing in New York City classified themselves as self-employed. The low percentage of Dominican entrepreneurs reported by the census data suggests that either the volume of economic enterprise among Dominicans is lower than empirical observation reveals or that a good portion of Dominican businesses simply operate within informal channels. None of the ethnographic studies conducted thus far has measured the rate of failure among the Dominican business owners nor the impact of the business class on the material well-being of the larger Dominican community. Conceivably one could explore whether the activities of small business owners might yield simply a margin of profit (in earnings as well as in indirect benefits) large enough to set them apart from the average Dominican worker. A question worth asking is whether entrepreneurship among Dominicans is likely to lead to effective capital accumulation, diversification, and expansion by surpassing the limitations imposed by the widespread poverty of the community that constitutes its primary clientele. These are, at any rate, some of the obstacles that stand before the aspirations of the Dominican business sector. Whether Dominican capitalists will follow the successful path trodden by Cuban capitalists, or the less glamorous role taken by Puerto Rican business is not yet entirely clear. When the monthly magazine *Hispanic Business* devoted its lead article in the March 1997 issue to Hispanic individuals or families whose wealth had reached at least $25 million, only one Dominican, the celebrated designer Oscar de la Renta, was included in the magazine's "Rich List." The list also featured seven Puerto Ricans and thirty-two Cubans. Whether or not these proportions remain the same among the rich, we can only hope that they will be more favorable among the small-scale entrepreneurs who are struggling to get a piece, even if a small one, of the American pie.

## VOLUNTARY ASSOCIATIONS

The origins of voluntary associations among Dominicans can be traced as far back as 1945 when fewer than 10,000 Dominicans lived in the United States. At the time, most Dominicans formed "expressive" or "affective" voluntary associations, many of which did not seek legal incorporation in the state. They began as networks of friends, acquaintances, and families. Most ethnographic research indicates that these organizations, defined as recreational and social, originally focused on celebrating family events (weddings, birthdays, and the like). Around 1962, they slightly shifted their interest by encompassing civic and cultural concerns such as the commemoration of important Dominican historical dates. Recent research, however, has begun to unveil the political nature of some of the early associations, which only ostensibly had recreational or social aims. Doña Carmen Bartolí, an active woman in some of the voluntary associations of the Dominican community of Washington Heights, came to New York City in 1945. She witnessed the development of some of these groups, particularly around Broadway, between 136th and 137th streets, an area she identifies as an active focus of Dominican political activity during the 1940s and 1950s. Some of these groups had been organized by people such as Carlito Suero who, after his exile in Cuba, had come to New York City to promote opposition to the Trujillo regime. While some of the organizations included avowed opponents of the dictator Rafael Léonidas Trujillo, other associations, formed around the end of 1961, were brought together by their pro-Trujillo sentiments after his assassination.

The two oldest surviving formal voluntary associations of Dominicans date back to the 1960s. The first, Centro Cívico Cultural Dominicano, was founded on December 14, 1962, and the second, Club Juan Pablo Duarte, on February 27, 1966. In 1989, following a suggestion made by President Joaquín Balaguer, Club Juan Pablo Duarte changed its name to Instituto Duartiano. The members felt that the word club could send the wrong message concerning the seriousness of the work of the association whose eponym, Juan Pablo Duarte, is the revered founding father of the Dominican nation. During the 1960s Dominicans formed nearly a dozen voluntary associations, and by the 1970s, with the heavy influx of new Dominican immigrants, this number had multiplied threefold. A pioneering study of voluntary associations among Dominicans residing in New York City found that in 1978 thirty-six of these associations existed in Washington Heights alone

(Sassen-Koob 1987). Most were just social clubs, but as early as 1974 there already existed organizations such as the Dominican Center for Orientation and Social Assistance, which was initially funded by a grant from the Episcopal Church to provide services in the areas of immigration, education, and counseling. Diego Delgado, its director, drew largely on a mostly volunteer staff. He hoped at the time "to develop a pilot project to gain more insights into the problems of Dominican newcomers in order to ameliorate their inhuman condition" (De Rege 1974: 8).

In many respects, Delgado's center is an ancestor to many of the well-known direct service community agencies that cater to Dominicans in New York, including Alianza Dominicana, which stood out in the 1990s as a vigorous organization with remarkable expertise in fund-raising as well as in garnering support from municipal, state, and federal levels of government. Alianza provides assistance to its clients in youth services, substance abuse prevention, recreation, employment training, education, and family services. The strongest of the direct-service agencies led by Dominicans in New York, Alianza began in the 1980s, when the formation of voluntary associations escalated. By the middle of the decade, their number had climbed to ninety in Washington Heights alone (Georges 1984; Sainz 1990).

As time went by, Dominicans began to form an ever larger number of "instrumental" associations such as Alianza Dominicana. These instrumental associations, generally defined as nonrecreational, nonexpressive, and goal-oriented, centered around self-help and advocacy. Asociaciones Dominicanas, founded in February 1974, and Asociación Comunal de Dominicanos Progresistas, founded on March 31, 1980, were among the leaders of the new kind of voluntary association. These organizations came into being to address the obstacles to the socioeconomic progress of Dominicans in New York City. Asociaciones Dominicanas originally intended to become a federation by grouping the various Dominican voluntary associations in the city. Its leaders thought a federation would allow them to address effectively the issues that concerned them. It soon became clear to its members, however, that for them to address the needs of the community for better jobs, education, and political empowerment, financial support was required, causing Asociaciones Dominicanas to change its orientation toward direct service. The fact that some of the members were professionals who had experience in dealing with city agencies and that others were college students in the city facilitated the transition as well as the acquisition of public funding.

Similarly, Asociación Comunal de Dominicanos Progresistas was born with the purpose of organizing Dominicans to fight for better social institutions (schools, housing, medical facilities) and overall community empowerment. Its founding members were all young Dominicans who had come to the United States as adolescents. They had been educated in U.S. schools and universities and had learned about the struggles for civil rights undertaken by Puerto Ricans and African Americans. In their statement of principles, the group identified Dominicans as a "national minority." They affirmed that Dominicans were not transitory visitors but permanent settlers, and that their concerns had to be defined around their needs and aspirations in the host country (Sainz 1990). Besides community organizing, the leadership felt that the association needed a service-oriented component that would allow them to participate actively not only in helping Dominicans to address their social needs, but also in designing the model and the philosophy under which to provide such help.

## MEMBERSHIP AND PARTICIPATION

There is no set way to determine the size of most associations. Problems such as lack of attendance records, fluctuations in the number of those who attend meetings, and the presence of people who, though classified as "friends of the association," share some of the responsibilities of the members make the numerical assessment of participants difficult. An association may have as few as 10 members or as many as 250. Their public events could draw the attendance of several hundreds. Associations, which are not service agencies, often require their members to pay dues. The amount ranges between $25 and $60 dollars per month or per year.

A prospective member is often required to fill out an application form which asks questions concerning the applicant's background, including job history, and time of arrival in the United States. New members are recommended or brought in by other members in good standing. Most associations require a new member to pass some sort of trial period (the length of time varies depending on the organization) in which character and interaction with others are observed by a membership committee. Incorporated associations tend to have strict admissions requirements and severe sanctions for members who violate the organization's code of conduct. These organizations safeguard themselves by scrutinizing applicants closely before granting membership. They screen meticulously those individuals who have been previously expelled from another organization.

Since many of the associations of the 1950s were in fact conducting subversive political activities, participation in many of these groups was highly selective and restricted to people who were of Dominican descent. Yet, this practice has changed in light of the rapid expansion of Dominicans in New

York City, their interrelation with other ethnic groups, and their interethnic familial ties through marriage. Furthermore, their social segregation fostered in many Dominicans a perception of themselves as a minority group that shared the plight of other minorities. As early as 1966, some Dominican associations began to open their doors to allow the participation of members from other national groups. In some cases, non-Dominicans not only enjoyed membership rights but actually ranked among the founding members of an association. Club Deportivo Dominicano and Centro Cultural Ballet Quisqueya were both founded by Dominicans in 1966, but since their very beginning, both organizations have included members who were not Dominican. Club Juan Pablo Duarte, on the other hand, began with a founding board of eleven members, including a Puerto Rican man.

Women have played a key leadership role in the development of voluntary associations among Dominicans, particularly in the early stages when only a handful of Dominicans lived in the United States and any community institution had to rely on both sexes in order to thrive. Women have ranged in their level of participation from as low as 20% in sports associations to as high as 75% in more general ones (Sainz 1990). They have also been instrumental in bringing people together to form associations. One of the best-known women activists in the community's voluntary associations is Ana Monción, who has served the Club Juan Pablo Duarte for several decades. Similarly, Club Cívico Cultural Dominicano was initiated by Doña Alfida, a woman who felt that Dominican culture had to be promoted in the host country. She believed that Dominicans should flaunt their cultural pride and disseminate their heritage among other groups. Women's activism is evident in that most associations, including direct-service agencies, rely on women volunteers to perform important tasks.

During the 1980s, however, many women became interested in developing gender-specific voluntary associations. This important development grew out of their dissatisfaction with their role in voluntary associations which failed to respond to the concerns of women in particular. Many women sensed that their talent was underutilized, and that they were often relegated to such activities as cooking, entertainment, decoration, and other tasks traditionally associated with women, but that their deepest concerns seldom came to the fore for discussion. In 1983 a group of activists got together to form the Asociación de Mujeres Dominicanas. The organization's leadership consisted mostly of women who had left traditional voluntary associations. They were young and many had higher education degrees from universities in the United States and in the Dominican Republic. The association chose to concentrate on issues of importance specifically to women in the United

States and in the homeland. Other organizations then emerged with the expressed purpose of tackling problems that affected strictly the life of Dominican women in the United States. One of the founding members in 1986 of Colectivo de Mujeres Dominicanas, Mirella Cruz, thought it necessary to separate the cause of Dominican women in the diaspora from those of the native land. She has argued that in the Dominican Republic women were on the vanguard organizationally. There they have established their voice in the debates on equal rights as well as other broad social concerns. But Dominican women in the United States are lagging behind, "still dealing with such basic issues as demanding the right to legitimacy, or gaining acceptance as spokespersons for the Dominican community." In keeping with the advent of gender-specific women's activism, several voluntary associations have emerged that cater to a female constituency, including the Dominican Women's Caucus, an organization whose members are mostly U.S.-born or U.S.-educated Dominican women. In the 1990s, the Dominican community housed thriving female-headed organizations like Centro de Desarrollo de la Mujer Dominicana, arguably the first direct-service agency created to serve specifically the needs of Dominican women.

## SOCIAL FUNCTION

Voluntary associations are perceived as institutions which could either facilitate or hamper the process of integration and socialization of an immigrant group. Early research among Dominicans led to the conclusion that, compared to other groups, Dominicans tended to form a larger number of "affective" rather than instrumental associations. Affective associations, viewed as resulting from an immigrant group's sense of uprooting, are venues whereby immigrants come together with their own to share their nostalgia for the home country. These associations are thought to do little to promote a healthy adaptation to the receiving society. Instead, they may actually foster cultural separateness, an ethnic isolationism that may harm the immigrant's process of integration into the new land. Subsequently, however, a higher number of instrumental associations among Dominicans has come into being. The change was produced in part by the overall proliferation of voluntary organizations as well as by the rise of various U.S.-educated Dominicans who have increasingly assumed their role as spokespersons of their community and who found in community organizations a fertile ground for promoting political and economic empowerment (Georges 1984). Instrumental associations are goal oriented. Among immigrants, they serve as a vehicle for ethnic constituencies to seek recognition in the eyes of the broader society in the host country. These associations aid in the process of integration of an immigrant group. Dominicans have already developed their share of them, laying, one hopes, an important foundation for the stability of the community.

## PROFESSIONALS AND ADVOCACY

The numerous advocacy organizations that have gained visibility among Dominicans over the last decade would give the impression that this community is one of the best organized ethnic groups in the United States. From business, to education, to labor, most areas of social concern have yielded specific organizations in the community. In New York alone, there is a Dominican Chamber of Commerce and a Dominican-American Chamber of Commerce. ICPARD-NY, the Dominican Authorized Public Accountants in New York Institute, boasts of a membership that exceeds 200 professionals. The leaders of the Dominican-American Travel Agents (DATA) claim to represent the overwhelming majority of Dominican travel agents who are active in the New York area. Dominican gypsy cab drivers, while not grouped under one single umbrella institution, have shown the ability to unite around common causes, such as the spread of violent attacks against drivers and the city's often inordinately restrictive regulation of their business. Even street vendors have organized effectively to the point of bringing their concern to City Hall and to the floor of the New York City Council.

The professional and advocacy organizations play a key role in enhancing the state of knowledge available about the Dominican community in the United States. Since each individual entity focuses on a differentiated area of interest and caters to a discrete constituency, it normally becomes also a resource center for data on that specific component of the Dominican community. Members of the Council of Dominican Educators and the Dominican Association of Education Professionals have gathered valuable data on the conditions of Dominican students and teachers in the public school system. The Dominican Youth Union, a school advocacy organization focusing on the needs of adolescents, has often organized activities to celebrate success among Dominican youngsters by honoring high school graduates who have been accepted into Ivy League universities. Working in collaboration with the Gregorio Luperón Preparatory School, an alternative intermediate school in northern Manhattan, and the City College of New York, the Dominican Youth Union has championed a precollege program that, in its third year (1997), registered over three hundred students. The Dominican Youth Union, headed by Ydanis Rodríguez, has become a resource for information about the condition of Dominican youths.

Although it is not nominally Dominican, the Northern Manhattan Coalition for Immigrant Rights has, by virtue of its location in Washington Heights, a clientele that is predominantly Dominican. Headed by a young U.S.-born Dominican lawyer named Manuel Matos, the coalition has played a salient role among the community's advocacy organizations. By the same token, the American Society of Dominican Attorneys, which includes many lawyers who are Dominican by birth or by descent, has rendered an equally valuable service by providing orientation to the community on immigration and legal matters. In a letter published in the Dominican newspaper *El Nacional* on December 8, 1996, Victor M. Espinal, a former president of the society, listed the names of eleven Dominican-descended lawyers who, he argued, deserved consideration by President Bill Clinton at the time of appointing federal judges for his second term in the White House. Six of the lawyers in the list already serve as judges at the state and municipal levels in New York, New Jersey, and Washington, D.C. Finally, the Dominican-American Professional Alliance (DAPA) announced its inauguration on June 14, 1997, and in the invitation brochure made known its mission "to utilize the resources and expertise of its professional members toward the betterment and growth of our Dominican community."

## EDUCATION

In the 1990 U.S. Census, it became clear that sectors of the population with a higher proportion of college education became richer while groups with large numbers of workers with less than high school education became poorer. Ramona Hernández, Francisco Rivera-Batiz, and Roberto Agodini established in their socioeconomic profile of Dominicans in New York that this community falls within the category of those who became poorer (1995: 33). According to these authors, "The Dominican population has a higher proportion of their labor force in unskilled, blue-collar jobs, a phenomenon associated with their lower educational attainment" (1995: 36). Table 3.7 gives figures that show at a glance the dismal situation of Dominicans in schooling vis-à-vis other ethnic groups in the city. This situation is particularly unfortunate in light of the technological changes in the workplace that during the 1980s reduced the demand for unskilled workers, shifting upward the demand for highly educated workers who could operate computers and other features of the technological age (41).

Concretely, the educational disadvantages that plague the Dominican community emanate not only from the low level of schooling that Dominican immigrants bring when they come to the United States. Equally important

Dominican professionals in New York City during a meeting with Santo Domingo and New York higher education officials. Courtesy of Dominican Studies Institute archives.

in this regard are the precarious services that Dominican children receive in the public schools they attend in New York. For instance, Community School District Six, the area that has the largest concentration of Dominican children in the classrooms, has one of the state's worst records, with math and reading scores that have given the community cause for serious concern. By the same token, George Washington High School, the secondary school of Washington Heights which, by virtue of its location, houses the greatest number of Dominican students, has one of the highest dropout rates in the entire United States. In 1996 Schools Chancellor Rudy Crew included George Washington among those that were to close due to the poverty of its performance. In 1997 a team of educators was convened to study the school's problems and to propose a model for its complete restructuring. Starting in September 1997 it was to be presented as a new school, and one will have to wait before judging the effect of the restructuring. What is at stake, clearly, is whether Dominican youngsters will have to continue attending schools that do a better job of crippling them intellectually and killing their hopes than of empowering them to face the challenges of a changing world.

However, irrespective of the precarious service that the public schools have been rendering them, a good number of Dominican youngsters have continuously graduated and managed to enter college. A report entitled *Immigration/Migration and the CUNY Student of the Future* (1995), published by the City University of New York, ranked Dominicans among the largest groups of foreign-born students admitted by the university. The report projects the continuation of that trend up to and beyond the year 2000. However, the report's predictions may be proved wrong in light of the structural changes undertaken by the university in 1996 that make it increasingly difficult for students to survive in the system if they require remediation or have limited English skills. The changes in the Human Resources Administration's application of the Welfare Law, which restricts the length of time that recipients of public assistance can remain in school; sharp tuition increases; and the changes marshaled by the new Board of Trustees of the City University of New York will most likely reduce the Dominican presence in the student body of the university.

Hope, of course, is not dead for Dominicans in education. Ever greater numbers of Dominicans are studying education and, upon graduation, seeking instructional and administrative positions in the public schools. There are already some Dominican school principals. As the members of the community continue to penetrate the schools, one may hope that they will soon be able to influence the system and to make it more responsive to the needs of Dominican students. Decisions that affect curriculum design, instruction, and leadership training may in years ahead be made with an eye on the well-being of the Dominican community, the largest share of the students entering the New York City public schools since the 1980s.

At the college level some gains can already be noted. In the majority of the City University campuses that have a significant Latino component in the student body, Dominicans tend to be the largest Latino subgroup. As a result of the Dominican presence, at least six of the City University campuses have created Dominican heritage survey courses. Some of the colleges have hired Dominican faculty, and the university has sponsored the creation of the CUNY Dominican Studies Institute, a research unit of the university housed at the City College campus. The purpose of the Dominican Institute is to create instruments of knowledge that will enhance the possibility of communication and will diminish the chances of tension between Dominicans and non-Dominicans in the United States. Toward that end, the Dominican Institute has organized over four conferences a year since it first started as a pilot project in the fall of 1992. It sponsors research on Dominican topics in various disciplines, and the results of those projects are subsequently published in the institute's Dominican Research Monographs. The

Children in a predominantly Dominican school district. © Josefina Báez.

Ramona Hernández, Silvio Torres-Saillant, and Ana García Reyes, three of the few Dominican faculty and staff of CUNY in 1995. Courtesy of Dominican Studies Institute archives.

institute commissioned the writing of *The Dominican Republic: A National History*, which appeared in 1995 under the authorship of historian Frank Moya Pons. With the publication of this volume, a survey of Dominican history from the colonial beginnings to the 1990s, the institute closed a previous bibliographic gap, since the only major Dominican history available in English in the United States until then had been *Naboth's Vineyard: The Dominican Republic (1844–1924)*, published in 1928 by American diplomat Sumner Welles.

With a more perceptible presence in higher education, Dominicans inevitably will become empowered with intellectual voices with which to echo the needs and aspirations of their community for full citizenship in the American society. There are already several scholars of Dominican descent who have access to academic forums which they have used to fend off vilification of the community. Worthy of note in that respect is the work of two Dominican junior scholars, doctoral candidates in the Sociology Department of the Graduate School and University Center of CUNY, who published an articulate rebuttal to the "welfare backlash" that they claim has recently been directed toward Dominicans. Ginetta Candelario and Nancy López contend that "the mythical welfare queen who looms so large in media and political discussions" does nothing but to shift "public attention away from real problems of structural social stratification to dissections of individual pathology" (1995: 20). They posit that any serious effort to lessen the "rates of Dominican households receiving public assistance" will have to begin by providing the community with "access to jobs that are better paying, more secure, and provide social benefit" (19). Candelario and López illustrate the fact that, armed with the intellectual weapons provided by education, the voice of the Dominican community will in the years ahead become louder and stronger and better able to demand that the community be granted the humanity that it is due.

## HEALTH ISSUES

The health condition of Dominicans in the United States, the majority of whom are young, requires a separate study. Little is known about their specific needs and problems other than what one might gather in general from their condition of social disadvantage. The following paragraphs present a limited overview of the state of Dominican health in body and mind. A therapist with ample experience in serving the psychological needs of immigrants in Washington Heights, where the majority of her clients were Dominicans, reported in 1980 that the two social classes that prevailed among Dominican immigrants both suffered psychological stress in their adopted New York home:

One class, with urban sophistication and some social connections, is now reduced to such menial tasks as washing dishes. The other class from an uneducated, rural background, is overwhelmed by bureaucracies, mass transit, etc. Even their children are prone to be misdiagnosed as retarded. For both these groups narcissistic injuries and anxieties often appear in somatic symptoms such as headaches, heart palpitations, dizziness, and sexual inhibitions. (Reubens 1980: 10).

The concept of narcissistic injuries refers to Heinz Kohut's theory of "self disorder" which psychologist Peggy Reubens uses to explain the plight of Dominicans. In Kohut's theory, people rely on healthy narcissism to carry them through the travails of life. Their cohesive sense of self "does not waver except under severe circumstances." Migration is such a severe circumstance. It causes "narcissistic injuries through loss of status and the loss of such self-objects as familiar surroundings and the persons or customs upon which much of a sense of self is based" (Reubens 1980: 10).

Years before the findings of Reubens, which she obtained while serving as director of the Washington Heights West Harlem Mental Health Clinic, another report suggested insights into the health and well-being of Dominicans. Looking at the case of a thirty-three-year-old Dominican immigrant named Juan Torres who, in 1973, ten years after his arrival from his native land, began having "seizure disorder," scholars Vivian Garrison and Claudewell Thomas undertook to place the man's condition in perspective. They examined the details of Juan's life in his native Cibao region, where he enjoyed respect among family and friends, as compared with his South Bronx apartment, where he not only lived humbly but suffered a reversal that deprived him of his status in his homeland. They pointed to the loss of power that may have led to his malady as a result of his being "most adversely affected economically and socially" or his being "least prepared and least able to cope" (Garrison and Thomas 1976: 247). Given the "subcultural management" that a return to good health would entail, they argued that American health care professions had little possibility of treating him successfully. Culturally, Juan and the U.S. mental health services "operate within separate and distinct systems—systems that simply do not mesh" (1976: 248).

One could probably draw insight about the health of the community from the fact that, in 1988, Washington Heights-Inwood, which served an area where Dominicans predominate, qualified for funding from the New York State Department of Health to set up a community-based cardiovascular disease prevention program—one of eight that received such grants in the state (Shea 1996: 166). Managed by a partnership of the Presbyterian Hospital, Teachers College of Columbia University, and the Columbia School of Public Health, the program set out to reduce the presence of cardiovascular disease risk factors, specifically smoking, sedentary lifestyle, obesity, hypertension, and hypercholesterolemia in the target community and thereby to reduce cardiovascular disease mordibity and mortality (1996: 167). The program lasted six years, during which it provided counseling, education, referrals, and training aimed at helping the community reduce the risk factors associated with cardiovascular disease. At the end of the sixth year, in 1994, the program transferred its resources to the community-based organization Dominican Women's Development Center. In their conclusions, the principal investigators advocate the continued funding of the project since "in poor, disadvantaged communities, such programs require on-going commitment of resources from external agencies, such as health departments, in order to be sustained" (170).

The above study makes no mention of alcohol consumption in the target area. It is, therefore, not known whether Washington Heights fits the profile advanced in 1978 by Andrew J. Gordon, who surveyed Dominicans in the

New England city of Newton, Massachusetts, and found that they did not exhibit problem drinking. According to Gordon, Dominicans were the exception to a prevalent tendency among "recent migrants of minority group status" who generally "experience alienation, increased reliance on alcohol, and consequently problem drinking" (Gordon 1978: 63). Among the members of the community studied by Gordon, drinking became less frequent and more moderate than it had been the custom for them in the Dominican Republic. The reasons explaining the change include the increased economic opportunities of Dominicans in Newton, the greater role of women in regulating the behavior of their men, a devaluation of the macho role that encourages unchecked drinking, and an "atomized social structure" that curtails the level of socializing outside the household.

One may take exception to Gordon's suggestion that Dominicans undergo a sort of cultural uplift in the United States, where "economic progress" stimulates "an austere and purposive comportment" as manifested in their adoption of "cultural ideas of discipline, sacrifice, and seriousness" that have a positive impact "on the family, on friendship, and on the community," marking sharp "contrasts with life in the Dominican Republic" (Gordon 1978: 81). He insinuates that Dominican ways need to be mended. But the scholar's peculiar causality notwithstanding, his findings can give the Dominican community a measure of consolation, especially if one can establish that Gordon's profile of Dominicans in Newton still holds true twenty years later and if it applies to Dominican immigrant settlements in New York and elsewhere in the United States. If so, the members of the community should be happy to know that there is at least one serious health problem that they do not have to worry about.

## DRUGS AND VIOLENCE

Dominicans have had to pay a price for the opportunity to come to the United States in search of fulfilling their aspiration to lead productive lives. The widespread poverty that afflicts them in the host country has made them prey to several social ills, including a high incidence of drug traffic in their midst and the violence and terror that invariably go along with it. Many Dominican youths have fallen under the spell of the drug industry, which deludes gullible minds with the promise of glamour and wealth. Too often they encounter death before completing their adolescence. As a result of the drug connection, Dominicans are overrepresented in the jails of the state of New York, whose justice system has a history of applying harsher sentences to minority defendants, as a study released by the administration of Governor George Pataki indicated in the fall of 1995 (Levy 1996: B1).

Since the illegal drug traffic has, over the last decades, become transnational, forging regional ties that defy borderlines, Dominican parents no longer enjoy the option of sending their children back home to keep them from getting into trouble, a strategy they often had recourse to in the 1970s and through the mid-1980s. At the same time they have had to endure the penury of seeing their community construed as a cause of the New York drug problem rather than as a victim of it. A *New York Post* journalist has spoken of Dominicans as "a community where three of the biggest sources of income are drugs, loan sharking, and money laundering" (McAlary 1991: 21). Mike McAlary, who seems intent on denouncing Dominican depravity, has painted the community thus: "The Dominican Republic has always exported talent to the United States. The sports pages are filled with statistics of Dominican baseball heroes in the Major Leagues. But for every George Bell and Pedro Guerrero, Stan Javier, and Julio Franco thrilling American audiences, there are now a dozen lethal drug dealers from San Francisco de Macorís terrorizing neighborhoods in upper Manhattan" (McAlary 1992: 3). With the backing of the *New York Post*, McAlary made a four-day trip to the Dominican Republic in order to get at the root of the crime problem among Dominicans. In San Francisco de Macorís, the city chosen for his sojourn, the journalist assessed the prevailing moral climate this way: "There is a hint of dark evil in every gold-toothed smile, and the sound of sinister laughter in the pock-marked streets" (1992: 3).

In addition to the print media, the journalist's report from his trip to the Dominican Republic reached the airwaves through a broadcast of "Inside Edition" on CBS. Dominican wrongdoing in New York subsequently became the subject of an NBC News report entitled "Immigration: The Good, the Bad, and the Illegal," which was broadcast nationally on Sunday, March 28, 1993. These examples suffice to illustrate the vulnerability of Dominicans in this country. For the time being, they have no means of challenging their detractors. The turning point will come, one may hope, when the Dominican community has accrued enough economic and political power to command respect. By then, perhaps, members of the community will have penetrated the media, and Dominicans with access to the columns of English-speaking newspapers and the cameras of mainstream television will have a say in the construction of their public image (Hernández and Torres-Saíllant 1996: 50).

The public image of Dominicans has spread into an oral tradition that has come to attribute to the community a special aptitude in the business of crime. A Puerto Rican woman bemoaning "the lack of a Puerto Rican criminal organization" is quoted as saying, "We don't sell drugs, we use them. The Italians, the Irish, the Cubans, and now the Dominicans each established effective, highly organized criminal operations" (Shorris 1992: 86). Dominicans are mentioned in the book *Latinos: A Biography of the People* by Earl Shorris for the most part in connection with crime. The author mentions Washington Heights primarily when narrating the adventures of characters such as J, who lives "on Audubon Avenue between 177th and 178th Streets, the supermarket of the Dominican-run drug business in New York" (1992: 254).

Shorris tells of the daily routines of Washington Heights drug dealers, their tenacity as they work long hours on the street, rain or shine, their interaction with area residents who are represented as colluding with the crime activity, and their devious strategies to keep their staff loyal (254–56). The dealers described by Shorris never buy for themselves anything that is flashy. They send their cash to the Dominican Republic, where they purchase comfort, but in the United States they simply work. When adversity meets them on the streets and the time comes for them to go to prison they take their losses (257). What seems indisputable is that the proliferation of drug dealing among Dominicans has to do with "high unemployment and diminishing resources especially for young people" as well as "the growth of a powerful and profitable multi-national drug industry" (Williams 1989: ix).

The cocaine industry in New York City, as we gather from an ethnographic study conducted by Terry Williams, relies mostly on "African-American and Latino boys and girls under eighteen," who generally come from severely low-income families in neighborhoods that have hardly a chance to rise above the poverty line. Many teenagers become involved "simply because they want jobs" (Williams 1989: 8). Dominican youngsters operated fifty of the fifty-three coke and crack houses visited by Williams for his ethnographic study of Washington Heights conducted in the 1980s. Dominicans outnumbered Puerto Rican, African American, and Colombian teenagers in the everyday transactions of the business. Their visibility, however, is inversely proportional to their real power. According to Williams, "Dominicans are the footsoldiers for the Colombians" (1989: 51). Irrespective of who actually controls the upper echelons of the industry, the notoriety of Dominicans in the streets has little correspondence to a corporate presence in the business.

At the same time, since the police have identified Washington Heights as a "hot spot" in the war on drugs, Dominican youngsters have suffered the most casualties (26). The perils of the industry, as was illustrated vividly in a *New York Times* article on the rise and fall of drug dealer José Reyes, include murderous battles with competitors, internecine rivalry, and clashes with law enforcement (McDonald 1996). The shadowy world of crack, cocaine, and heroin puts Dominican youngsters face to face with the constant menace of incarceration or death. The community, though, does not yet have a solid reason to despair about the involvement of their youth in this dangerous crime activity. Nobody has yet documented the numerical significance of Dominican drug dealers in proportion to the size of the community. No real basis exists to suppose that the percentage of Dominicans connected with the industry exceeds that of any other of the communities afflicted with the drug problem, which is neither ethnic nor nationality specific. It is a social problem of the United States.

## POLITICAL EMPOWERMENT

Dominicans have not, on the whole, made any major political strides since their population began to grow rapidly in the mid-1960s. But their moderate gains thus far give grounds for holding an optimistic outlook on the future role that Dominicans might play in state and municipal politics in New York and elsewhere in the years to come. At present, however, the community suffers from a political invisibility that is hardly justifiable in light of the great size of the Dominican population. Among other impediments to their visibility, Dominicans face the challenge of dismantling the widespread perception among elected officials and other policy makers that "Dominicans don't vote," which makes them appear expendable in the eyes of legislators. Howard Jordan, a keen observer of the political scene, has offered valuable testimony to this effect. In 1987 he failed to get a favorable response from any of the more than thirty State Assembly members whom he approached to enlist their support of a bill that sought to address the needs of New York's Dominicans: "Political doors were slammed—or closed ever so gently—on our lobbying efforts on behalf of a community without clout" (Jordan 1997: 37).

At this writing, in 1997, a decade after Jordan's frustrated lobbying effort, the notion of Dominicans as politically insignificant may still prevail, evidence to the contrary notwithstanding. Angelo Falcon and Christopher Hanson Sánchez, the authors of *Latino Immigrants and Electoral Participation*, a study released by the Institute for Puerto Rican Policy in July 1996, showed that Dominicans had meaningful registration and turnout rates in municipal elections in 1992 and 1993. In 1993 they made up 11% of total Latino registered voters and 2% of registered voters in the entire New York City population. In 1992 and 1993 Dominican votes accounted for 13.3% and

12.1% of all the votes actually cast by Latinos. The authors of the study suggest that "successful candidates from one's own racial-ethnic group and the resources they bring to the registration process is an important factor" in fostering participation. If that claim is correct, one may expect a significant increase of the number of Dominicans casting their ballots at the polls now that Dominican elected officials have begun to surface in the municipal and state legislatures.

Concomitantly, the number of Dominicans who are eligible to vote is increasing at a rapid pace. According to *The Newest New Yorkers: An Analysis of Immigration into New York City during the 1980s*, a 1992 study issued by New York City's Department of City Planning, immigrants from the Dominican Republic ranked ninth in the country among all foreign nationals who became naturalized as U.S. citizens during the 1980s. In New York State, they led all other foreign-born communities in their rate of naturalization. From empirical observation in the mid-1990s, one could attend swearing-in ceremonies of the Immigration and Naturalization Service in New York City and note that the majority of those taking the oath of citizenship were often Dominican. Moreover, the ascent of the Republicans in the U.S. Congress has fueled the impetus of the community to naturalize. Put briefly, the Newt Gingrich "revolution" has given added currency to anti-immigrant sentiments nationwide to the point that many Dominicans have come to believe that only citizenship can safeguard them from deportation. Ironically, fear, which has caused many in the community to rush to file for citizenship to protect themselves from impending doom, has also increased the potential of Dominicans to make a difference as a new political force.

The first indicators of empowerment for Dominicans surfaced in the 1980s, when several members of the community joined various local governance bodies. As Jordan has noted, six Dominicans had been elected to the Area Policy Board, and four obtained appointments to the Community Planning Board in Washington Heights. Two Dominicans won election to the position of Democratic District Leader: María Luna, a woman who had attained the support of the Democratic party machinery in Upper Manhattan's 72 Assembly District, and Julio Hernández, a man who managed to win without party machinery backing. Similarly, members of the community participated actively in the debates about the implementation of the new city charter in 1991 and the redrawing of the city's electoral maps, which culminated in the creation of City Council district No. 10, which housed a majority of Dominican voters. Among the visible participants in that process was Fernando Lescaille, a founding member of an ad-hoc political advocacy

Dominican-born New York City Council member Guillermo Linares (right) in the company of Professor Francisco Rivera Batiz (center) and former Assemblyman John Brian Murtaugh. Courtesy of Dominican Studies Institute archives.

organization called Northern Manhattan Committee for Fair Representation and the president of the Dominican Public Policy Project (Jordan 1997: 40).

The creation in 1991 of the new district in Washington Heights led to an electoral contest that featured four Dominicans as the most prominent runners: Guillermo Linares, María Luna, Adriano Espaillat, and Apolinar Trinidad. Linares won the election and became the first Dominican council member in New York City. Simultaneously, on the other bank of the Hudson River, Kay Palacios, the U.S.-born daughter of Dominican parents, won a seat as a council member in a New Jersey municipality. Afterward, Linares succeeded at several reelection efforts, unlike Palacios, who remained active as president of the Hispanic Business and Professional Association in New Jersey. In November 1996, Adriano Espaillat became the first Dominican to serve in the New York State Assembly, after unseating John Brian Murtaugh, an Irish-descended incumbent who had held his post in Manhattan's 72 district for sixteen years.

There is much speculation about what lies in store for Dominicans in politics. Jordan has spoken of the emergence of "a growing disunity among Dominican political elites" as an obstacle to the community's political empowerment (1997: 41). Many view with concern the possibility that another Dominican might challenge Councilman Linares or Assemblyman Espaillat in upcoming elections, fearing that such internal competition may tear the community asunder. A more optimistic interpretation would be that if two Dominicans run for the same office, the community will have to justify their vote on the basis of other than strictly ethnic loyalties. Dominicanness would not suffice. The candidate would have to show substance, a real platform, and maintain a clear record. But, most important, the community should not think that it may only hold accountable those legislators who are Dominican. As the community raises its awareness about its own ability to influence the political process, it may begin to show legislators, Dominican and non-Dominican, Latino and non-Latino, that the pretext "Dominicans don't vote" can no longer be invoked with political impunity.

## NOTES

1. These figures stem from the following data. During the 1970s less than 50% of Dominicans reported having an occupation before migrating to the United States. The numbers given in each pertinent year by the INS annual reports were 46.8% in 1970, 36.5% in 1973, 35.7% in 1974, 29.3% in 1975, 28% in 1976, and 35.4% in 1977. In 1982, out of 17,451 Dominicans admitted, only 6,216 reported having had an occupation before migrating to the United States. The number of people who did not report an occupation before migration included housewives, children, and others.

2. For the sake of convenience, here we look at Dominicans in comparison with other Hispanics, non-Hispanic whites, non-Hispanic blacks, and New York City overall.

**4**

# *Forging a Dominican-American Culture*

## DOMINICAN INVISIBILITY

The state of knowledge about the cultural expressions and contributions of Dominicans in the United States is precarious. Dominicans are generally left out of most reference publications that purport to account for the ethnic groups that make up the American people. They have often been left out even of sources dealing specifically with the Hispanic portion of the U.S. population. Over four decades ago, a book entitled *Spanish-Speaking People in the United States*, while making no mention of Dominicans, focused on Mexican Americans, Hispanos of New Mexico, and Puerto Ricans; it even designated Filipinos as Hispanics (Burma 1954). Nearly twenty years later, the Spanish-speaking American chapter of a guide to media and materials covering American ethnic minorities still omitted Dominicans, limiting the survey to Cubans, Puerto Ricans, and Mexican Americans or Chicanos (King 1976: 189–239). In the same year, the bibliographic compendium *A Comprehensive Bibliography for the Study of American Minorities* carried a section entitled "From the Islands," which included the "Puerto Rican-American Experience" and the "Cuban American Experience" but made no mention of Dominican life in the United States (Miller 1976, vol. 2: 757 et passim). Still in the 1990s the place accorded to Dominicans in reference sources remained so meager that it seemed possible to compile a voluminous *Hispanic Almanac* covering virtually every field of endeavor and to give no more than five pages to Dominican personalities and events (Kanellos 1994).

The invisibility of Dominicans in the reference sources seems difficult to explain since "Dominicans constitute the fourth largest Hispanic group in the United States" (Carrasquillo and London 1993: 37). Nor do they differ from other Latinos in terms of the goals that brought them to this country. They came primarily in search of jobs and opportunities. By the same token, they resemble other Hispanics in the barriers and obstacles that on occasion block their aspirations: insufficient English language proficiency and lack of job skills. Like their Cuban, Puerto Rican, and Mexican/Chicano counterparts, "Parents of Dominican children confront social, educational, and economic needs: housing, jobs, English language competence, cultural adjustment, formal education or vocational training, and financial and legal assistance" (1993: 137).

Dominicans arrived in the United States en masse in the mid-1970s, excluding, that is, the small but meaningful groups of Dominicans who came prior to the great exodus, and they have always tried to build homes, earn a living, find meaning in the world, create communities, and, ultimately, secure the future of their children. They have not sat idly. Their invisibility in the reference sources does not correspond to a quiet passivity on their part. Dominicans have not secluded themselves nor have they shied away from public view. Witness the fact that, since the founding of the first Dominican Parade in 1982 in New York City, every year in August well over 150,000 people have come to Manhattan to celebrate Dominicanness and display many of the community's cultural traditions. By now such massive Dominican gatherings have proliferated. In 1990 a community activist named Felipe Febles organized the Gran Parada y Carnaval Dominicanos de El Bronx, another parade that has become institutionalized in the Bronx county, rallying thousands of Dominicans to march on July of every year. There is another Dominican parade in Haverstraw, New York, as well as equivalent annual gatherings in New Jersey and Connecticut.

Dominicans also congregate around cultural and sports institutions. There is a Casa Dominicana in Chicago, Illinois, with counterparts in Boston, Massachusetts, in Providence, Rhode Island, and in various cities of New York, New Jersey, Florida, and Connecticut. Invariably those "cultural houses" provide a suitable place for people in the community to hear lectures on various Dominican topics or to enjoy presentations or exhibits involving artists from the homeland or from the diaspora. Additionally, "community clubs" (*clubes comunales*) abound in Dominican neighborhoods. Already in 1985 the organizing committee of the Dominican Parade in Manhattan listed 125 such formal associations in New York city alone. A "partial" listing of "Dominican Associations in the United States" appearing in a 1994 doctoral dissertation included 109 organizations (Goris-Rosario 1994: 97–99). Similarly, the community exhibits much activism in the area of print media. Neighborhoods teem with Dominican newspapers, a combination of those imported from the Dominican Republic and those put out by small immigrant publishers for local distribution. A Dominican journalist from the community who surveyed print media found over one hundred Dominican weekly, monthly, and other periodical publications that have come into existence in New York alone since 1950, when two anti-Trujillo Dominican writers started the paper *Patria* to promote anti-Trujillo views among the exile community (Cruz Almánzar 1993: 79–88).

Dominicans have also made themselves visible in professional sports, chiefly in major league baseball. Starting with Osvaldo Virgil, who joined the New York Giants in 1956, the Dominican Republic has become a regular source of talent for baseball teams. Baseball fans in the United States are familiar with Juan Marichal, Manuel Mota, César Cedeño, Ricardo Carty, Pedro Guerrero, and Joaquín Andújar, as well as Felipe, Mateo, and Jesús Alou. The Dominican Republic now exports baseball talent just as it formerly exported sugar, to borrow the analogy used by scholar James Loucky. Dominican players have had an extraordinary impact on professional baseball in the United States insofar as no less than 6% of all players and close to 50% of all foreign players in the major leagues are Dominican (Loucky 1992: 956). The impact of Dominican players manifests itself most notably in that many major league teams have identified the Dominican Republic as an important source for the grooming and recruitment of future baseball stars. Toward that end, they have set up baseball academies in various Dominican cities:

Not unlike colonial outposts, academies serve as talent banks for identifying and signing prospects, with bonuses averaging less than $5,000, compared to over $50,000 in the United States. They also function as socialization agents for developing not only athletic skills, but even more importantly, the mental aspects of the game, some knowledge of English, and an understanding of the psychological adjustments required for surviving in a foreign system. (Loucky 1992: 957)

Significantly, though, direct contact between U.S. major league teams and Dominicans in their homeland reduces the role that Dominicans from the United States could have in the sport. When we think of Dominicans in baseball, it is normally the sending society rather than the immigrant community that comes to mind. Only recently have a few Dominican youths from the diaspora inserted themselves successfully in major league baseball. But, in general, that sport remains the province of recruits from the academies in the homeland. In that respect, the achievement of someone like the academy recruit José Rijo, named Most Valuable Player of the 1990 World Series, means less for U.S. Dominicans than the stardom of someone like St. John's University's basketball player Felipe López, an offspring of the immigrant community. The child of a humble Dominican immigrant couple, López rose from the classrooms of New York City high schools to become a sports celebrity of national stature. His movement up from the "hood," as it were, suggests to U.S. Dominican youngsters a model of individual excellence that they can identify with more easily than those cases in which the successful player is a talent imported from the Dominican Republic. At any rate, as the foregoing milestones should indicate, Dominicans in the United States have lived, experienced, and created enough to justify a greater cultural visibility than they now enjoy. Also, they have forged cultural forms that differ from the Dominican traditions brought from the sending country as well as from those found in the receiving society. The pages that follow will attempt to map, in a necessarily sketchy way, the presence of Dominicans in the United States in scholarship, literature, performing and visual arts, popular music, religion, and entertainment.

## THE NINETEENTH CENTURY

The presence of Dominicans in the United States in the realm of social and cultural expressions stretches back to the nineteenth century when prominent enemies of the government or revolutionaries committed to the regional struggle for the independence of the Greater Antilles made their way to North America. Dissidents from the Dominican Republic have chosen the United States as a haven since the 1830s when Juan Pablo Duarte, the founding father of Dominican nationhood, spent time in New York before finally arriving in Santo Domingo to activate the cause of national independence (R. Duarte 1994: 40). Decades later, a less venerable Dominican political figure, the treacherous President Buenaventura Báez, found himself in the United States more than once. On June 13, 1866, he wrote from St. Thomas to his brother Damián Báez and asked him to arrange a meeting for him in New York with some potential business associates (Rodríguez Demorizi 1969: 459). In a February 5, 1867, letter to a friend's daughter named Corinne, he spoke about his having just arrived in Curaçao from New York (1969: 203). On December 25, 1875, in a letter written from Curaçao to Damián, the shrewd caudillo complained about his having been detained "in New York when I was there having my eye illness treated" (465).

But not all Dominicans who lived in the United States were prominent political figures who came seeking refuge or support to advance overseas causes. For instance, Captain José Gabriel Luperón, an older brother of the highly regarded Dominican patriot General Gregorio Luperón, came to the United States to participate in the American Civil War, fighting on the side of the Union troops. Dominican sources state that he distinguished himself in battle, earning a promotion to the rank of captain, which was conferred upon him by President Abraham Lincoln himself. He played a decisive role in the successful entry of Union naval vessels into the Mississippi (Rodríguez Demorizi 1963: 185). Another case, that of Juan de Dios Tejada who resided in New York with his wife Altagracia Frier and their four children toward the end of the century, suggests that in the nineteenth century some Dominican families did consider settling in this country as one of their options. Tejada's family met a tragic end. On a trip to Santo Domingo their ship capsized, resulting in the death of Altagracia and the four children. Some time later, as one learns from an extant letter of his dated December 24, 1897, Tejada remarried and sought to rebuild his life in his adopted city of New York (Tejada 1994: 281–83).

## THE EARLY TWENTIETH CENTURY

The individual cases of Dominicans living in this country, particularly in New York, already amounted to an appreciable presence by the beginning of the twentieth century. That much at least can be gathered from the testimony of the renowned philologist Pedro Henríquez Ureña who arrived in the city on January 30, 1901, at the age of sixteen. His father, Dr. Francisco Henríquez y Carvajal, brought him and his older brother Fran, to be joined later by his younger brother Max, so that they could study in New York under the "influence of a superior civilization" (Roggiano 1961: xii). According to Pedro's testimony, they found "various Dominicans" upon arriving in New York:

the ex President D. Alejandro Woss y Gil, a man of subtle intelligence and good friend of my father as well as of my cousin Enrique, the Consul Leonte Vásquez, brother of the then Vice President Horacio; the students Floricel Rojas and *Niño* Alfonseca; that remarkable character Abelardo A. Moscoso, an energetic man, not entirely uncouth but of somewhat bizarre ideas and feelings on account of his long years of struggle in exile; and many more whom we had less to do with. (cited in Roggiano 1961: xiii)

Pedro and his brother took courses at Columbia University, lived in the vicinity of the campus, and frequented the libraries as well as the theaters of the city. As a regular feature of their social life, they also visited, in addition to educational and cultural institutions, "the hotels and houses that lodged the Dominicans who came to New York for their summer vacation, whose number increased every year" (Roggiano 1961: xxviii). On April 26, 1902, they received the news that their father, having lost his government position, could no longer provide for them as students abroad and urged them to return home. However, the young men, with a temerity befitting their youth, chose to stay in New York. Max, the youngest of the three brothers, subsequently recalled their choice thus: "My brothers and I decided to find a way to make a living in New York: Fran and Pedro found employment as retail sales workers, and I got a temporary job as a pianist in a restaurant" (M. Henríquez Ureña 1950: xxxv). Their determination to stay in New York provides us with a case of young Dominicans fending for themselves in the big city at the very beginning of the present century. In 1903 the young men rented their own flat, one located on West 15th Street in Manhattan, where other compatriots would board as well: Virgilio Ortea, a family friend who had come to New York "to work in commerce," and his brother Julio, whose parents had sent him so that he could "become Americanized" (Roggiano 1961: xxix). They lived in a neighborhood that "teemed with Dominican exiles who now increasingly headed for New York" (1961: xxxi).

His brothers having left before him, Pedro departed from the United States in 1904. He would come back a decade later to serve in Washington, D.C. as a foreign correspondent of the Cuban newspaper *Heraldo de Cuba*. During his second North American sojourn, Henríquez Ureña also contributed columns to *El Fígaro*, another Cuban paper. His stay in Washington lasted until May 1915, when he relocated to New York in order to join the editorial staff of the weekly *Las Novedades*, a cultural and commercial publication founded months earlier by the Dominican lawyer, publicist, and intellectual Francisco J. Peynado. The success of *Las Novedades* gave Pedro's own father the idea years later that perhaps he and his sons could set up a company in New York dedicated to the publication and distribution of books in Spanish (Henríquez y Carvajal 1994: 657). They did not bring the idea to fruition, but their projection, aided by the example of Peynado's business venture, suggests that nearly forty years before the start of the great exodus, there were already Dominicans who conceived of New York as a ground for economic advancement.

Early in 1916 Pedro began teaching at the University of Minnesota, in Minneapolis, while pursuing graduate studies at the same institution. He obtained first an M.A. degree and soon thereafter a Ph.D. In the same commencement exercises of June 1918 in which his doctorate was conferred, his sister Camila Henríquez Ureña also received a graduate degree, an M.A. in Spanish literature. Shortly after receiving their diplomas, Pedro and Camila left the United States to accept academic appointments elsewhere: he in Spain, Mexico, and Argentina; she in Cuba. After resigning from his faculty position at the University of Minnesota, Pedro returned to this country two decades later, this time to Cambridge, Massachusetts, to assume a Visiting Professorship at Harvard University during academic year 1940–1941. Apart from his teaching duties, the post included delivering the prestigious Charles Eliot Norton Lectures. In these talks, which he gave originally in English, he undertook to trace "the search for expression" in the literary production of the Hispanic Americas from the colonial period to 1940.

## INDIVIDUAL DOMINICANS IN THE UNITED STATES

Some Dominicans, as we have seen, distinguished themselves in this country in various fields of endeavor during the earlier half of the twentieth century. To a large extent, the famous designer Oscar de la Renta followed in their footsteps. Born in Santo Domingo on July 22, 1932, de la Renta traveled to Europe following his secondary school studies. In Madrid he discovered his talent for fashion illustration, and his work soon attracted the attention of Spanish designer Cristóbal Balenciaga. In 1962 he went to Paris, where he became associated with the couture house of Christian Dior. The following year he came to settle in New York City, and since then he has become a household name in the United States. Naturalized a U.S. citizen in 1971, de la Renta, who has "practically cornered the U.S. on splendid evening clothes" and "is the first American ever to take over a French couture business," enjoys the friendship of many of the most famous, wealthiest Americans from Henry Kissinger to Brooke Astor to Isaac Stern (Duffy 1993: 68, 70). De la Renta and his wife, Annette Reed, "popularly considered heir to the title of doyenne of New York society currently held by Brooke Astor," have played visible roles in many of the most prestigious cultural institutions of the city. Reed serves as a member of the board of trustees of the New York Public Library and vice chairperson of the board of trustees of the Metropolitan Museum of Art, and de la Renta sits on the boards of the Metropolitan Opera, Carnegie Hall, and the Americas Society (Novas 1995: 66).

Particularly during the first half of the twentieth century, a good number of people from the Dominican Republic headed for the United States in pursuit of individual dreams. Official statistics give an average of 970 Dominicans legally entering this country per year from 1950 through 1960

(Moya Pons 1994: 6). For the most part, these individuals enjoyed a level of social advantage in their home country. They had the necessary influence to obtain permission to travel abroad at a time when the totalitarian regime that ruled the nation tried zealously to prevent emigration. They also could afford the expenses involved in relocating to a foreign metropolis without the support system of an ethnic enclave that spoke their language and facilitated their way to gainful employment. Invariably, the Dominicans who came prior to 1960 tended to be light skinned, not only because of the prevalence of antiblack feelings in the United States at the time, but also because the Dominican Republic's negrophobic government favored lighter-skinned applicants when authorizing travel abroad.

Manuel de Moya, a tall, well-built, Caucasian-looking Dominican, was earning his living as a male model in New York City when the dictator Rafael Leónidas Trujillo came to the city on a diplomatic errand during the 1940s. The tyrant admired the young man's good looks when he saw his picture on a printed advertisement, and he was pleasantly surprised to learn that the model was a Dominican. Trujillo had Moya found and brought to him speedily, after which he made Moya a job offer that the ambitious young man could not refuse. Moya traveled back to the Dominican Republic and there became an influential member of Trujillo's cabinet. Other notable Dominicans who lived in the United States in the 1940s included the grandparents, parents, and other relatives of the writer Julia Alvarez. Her parents met and married in the United States, hence Julia's birth in New York City in 1950. In fact, Mrs. Alvarez, the author's mother, came from a family with deep roots in the United States. The writer's "maternal uncles and maternal aunts were sent to American boarding schools, and her uncles then went to Ivy League universities" (Novas 1995: 426).

The two Dominicans who attained the greatest visibility in the United States during the first half of the present century were María Montez and Porfirio Rubirosa. Born in the southwestern city of Barahona to well-to-do parents on June 6, 1912, María Africa Gracia Vidal married William G. McFeeters, a British Army officer who headed the Barahona branch of the National City Bank of New York (Vicens de Morales 1993: 3). After having lived in Ireland for eight years, she arrived in New York City on July 3, 1939, to try her luck as a model under the name of Marie McFeeters. With her mind passionately set on becoming "a great star," she landed a contract with Universal Studios in 1940, moved to Hollywood, and changed her name to María Montez. She had a major part in the movie *Arabian Nights* (1942), which made her a Hollywood darling, and she played the title role in *Cobra Woman* (1943), which elevated her to "world cult status" (Susann 1994: 4).

Her stardom did not last. A move to Paris with her second husband, the French actor Jean Pierre Aumont, estranged her from Hollywood. She was looking forward to a Hollywood comeback when death surprised her in 1951. Known affectionately in her day as "the Queen of Technicolor," more than four decades after her death she remains "the object of an extensive fan cult thirsting for nostalgia and high camp" (Kanellos 1994: 552). Her other film credits include *Bowery to Broadway* (1944), *Gypsy Wildcat* (1944), *Sudan* (1945), *Tangier* (1944), *The Exile* (1947), and *Pirates of Monterey* (1947).

Porfirio Rubirosa (1909–1965), on the other hand, had already achieved a reputation as an international playboy when he made his way to the New York jet set in the late 1940s. Having married and divorced Flor de Oro Trujillo, the first-born daughter of the Dominican dictator, he retained the friendship and support of his former father-in-law, the powerful benefactor who enabled him to finance a life of luxury and romantic indulgence. In France, Rubirosa charmed the actress Danielle Darrieux, leading to a marriage that lasted for only a little while, after which, in the United States, he successfully wooed Doris Duke, a wealthy member of the Duke family, the tobacco magnates and philanthropists after whom Duke University in Durham, North Carolina, is named. In 1952, while representing the Trujillo regime in a diplomatic capacity in New York, Rubirosa began a highly publicized love affair with the Hollywood actress Zsa Zsa Gabor, whose sister Eva Gabor, also a show business celebrity, would become his wife years later. The Dominican frolicker found his way into another wealthy American family on December 30, 1953, when he wedded Barbara Hutton, the granddaughter of Frank Winfield Woolworth, founder of the general merchandise store chain that numbered more than a thousand branches throughout the United States and abroad ("Rubirosa, Porfirio" 1986: 158–59).

## DOMINICANS IN THE UNITED STATES AS EXILES

Like Rubirosa, a fairly good number of the Dominicans who resided in the United States prior to the 1960s were government agents, diplomats, adventurers, entrepreneurs, or students from wealthy families. But probably a larger number was made up of political exiles and expatriates who opposed or had incurred the enmity of the ruling structure in the homeland. The government that generated the best-known, most active community of expatriates was no doubt the thirty-year-long ruthless dictatorship of Trujillo, which made it gravely dangerous for dissidents to remain at home. Exiled Dominicans organized anti-Trujillo campaigns abroad and formed opposition parties in various foreign cities. The best known of those parties, Partido

Revolucionario Dominicano (PRD), had an important headquarters in New York, led by notable leaders of the resistance. Nicolás Silfa, a prominent antagonist of the dictatorship who for years headed the New York chapter of the PRD, has recorded in his memoirs *Guerra, traición y exilio* (1980) a useful account of the anti-Trujillo struggle of Dominicans in the United States at the time.

The importance of New York as an arena for Dominican patriots committed to combating the tyrannical regime of their homeland is attested to by the Dominican government's efforts to extend its persecution of dissenters to this city, which became the stage for many brutal murders. In 1935 opposition leader Angel Morales lived with his roommate Sergio Bencosme in an apartment located at 87 Hamilton Place in uptown Manhattan. One day their landlady, Carmine Higgs, saw a gunman break in asking for Morales. The hired killer, identified later as Luis de la Fuente Rubirosa, came upon Bencosme and, mistaking him for Morales who was not at home, shot him to death (Hicks 1946: 55–56). Another Trujillo opponent, the novelist Andrés Requena, who had authored the antigovernment novel *Cementerio sin cruces*, met his end at 243 Madison Avenue in Manhattan's East Side on October 2, 1952. The Dominican consul in New York had led him deceitfully to this place, where he was ambushed by mercenaries of the dictatorship (Miolan 1985: 56). The consul was the sanguinary Felix W. Bernardino, who had previously threatened to shoot him "under any lamp-post in New York," according to a testimony by Requena himself found after the murder ("The Galíndez Mystery and the Trujillo Horror" 1956: 3). Bernardino's boisterous aggression was emulated at times by his sister, Ambassador Minerva Bernardino, who ironically went on to receive periodic honors for humanitarian service after the end of the dictatorship. She once shrieked at the journalist and author Wenzell Brown, "If Trujillo doesn't kill you, my brother will," according to an article published by Brown in the May 1956 issue of *Look* magazine. Ms. Bernardino had been represented unflatteringly as a vicious Trujillo lackey in the Dominican chapter of Brown's *Angry Men, Laughing Men* (1947).

None of Trujillo's murders in New York elicited as much publicity as that of the Basque exile Jesús de Galíndez who for six years had lived in the Dominican Republic, where he taught and served as a consultant in Trujillo's Ministry of Labor and Foreign Affairs. Separating himself from the Dominican government, Galíndez came to New York. Here he obtained a doctoral degree at Columbia University with a dissertation entitled "The Era of Trujillo," an inside story that revealed the madness, the corruption, and the criminality of the regime. When word reached Trujillo that the exposé would soon appear in book form, he took revenge. Cuban journalist Manuel de Dios Unanue wrote that it was Ms. Bernardino who took it upon herself to inform the tyrant about the book, emphasizing the harm it would do him and inciting him to take action (Unanue 1982: 129). On March 12, 1956, after finishing his lecture at Columbia University, Galíndez was abducted by Trujillo's agents and flown back to Santo Domingo, where, it is said, the tyrant personally saw him to his death (Miolán 1985: 57; "The Galíndez Mystery" 1956: 3). The crime sparked the outrage of the international community, and the good offices of Franklin D. Roosevelt, Jr., the former president's son, as counsel of the Dominican government, were needed to help assuage the discredit of the Trujillo regime in the United States.

## DOMINICAN-AMERICAN LITERATURE

Despite the apparent resistance of historians and compilers of U.S. Hispanic literature to include Dominican authors in their panoramic vistas, as illustrated by *The Hispanic Literary Companion* (Kanellos 1997) and *The Latino Reader* (Augenbraum and Fernández Olmos, 1997), there has been a Dominican literary presence in the United States since the turn of the century. Pedro Henríquez Ureña, who would subsequently become a towering figure of Latin American letters, began his literary career here in a formal way. A good portion of his professional development took place in this country. Here he obtained academic degrees, taught at the University of Minnesota and Harvard University, and produced a sizable portion of his literary texts. His sister, the scholar Camila Henríquez Ureña, completed her graduate studies at the University of Minnesota in 1918. Subsequently, she taught literature at Vassar College in Poughkeepsie, New York, from 1941 through 1958. On or about 1914, the Dominican entrepreneur and intellectual Francisco J. Peynado founded the cultural weekly *Las Novedades*, which opened its pages to many Dominican writers who lived in New York.

Among the well-known Dominican poets and short fiction writers who lived and worked in New York at the time, José M. Bernard (1873–1954) published a volume of verse entitled *Renuevos* (1907) through a printing company called Imprenta Hispano-Americana. The following year, the poet and short story writer Fabio Fiallo (1866–1942), a renowned author who befriended many of the major literary figures of Latin America, including the great Nicaraguan poet Rubén Darío, published a volume of short fiction entitled *Cuentos frágiles* (1908). Then in 1915, Manuel Florentino Cestero (1879–1926), another highly regarded name in Dominican literature, published the book of poems *El canto del cisne*, at the print shop of *Las Novedades* in New York, and five years later he published a prose fiction work entitled *El amor en Nueva York.*

Then came the three decades of the ruthless Trujillo dictatorship (1930–1961), a period during which many writers who did not feel comfortable about investing their creative talents in justifying the crimes of the government and praising the tyrant, which was the function of those who lived under the regime, had no other choice but to leave the country. Many migrated to the United States, particularly New York. Among the best known were Andrés Requena (1908–1952), Angel Rafael Lamarche (1899–1962), and Hector J. Díaz (1910–1952). Requena wrote in New York the novel *Cementerio sin cruces* (1951), which he published in Mexico under Editorial Veracruz. Lamarche wrote in New York the short fiction collection *Los cuentos que Nueva York no sabe* (1949), published at Talleres Gráficos La Carpeta, also in Mexico. Less is known about the verse produced in New York by Díaz during the last years of his life. It has yet to be determined which portion of the complete verse of Díaz, the Dominican poet whose work is most often recited by nonliterary audiences, corresponds to his stay in the United States.

With the great exodus that followed the death of Trujillo in 1961, and the chain of events that the demise of the dictator unleashed for the next few years, culminating in the civil war of 1965 and the U.S. military invasion that ensued, the socioeconomic and cultural profile of Dominicans in this country changed radically. Dominican immigrants no longer came exclusively from the economic, intellectual, and political elites that opposed the regime or from the light-skinned, well-to-do families whose relative social privilege made foreign travel accessible to them. Now international migration was open to all. As the migratory flow quickened, poor peasants and residents of urban ghettoes far outnumbered the middle-class immigrants who had arrived earlier. The Dominican community in the United States thus became increasingly darker and poorer, while the industrial economy enjoyed by earlier immigrants lost the ability to incorporate new workers. As a result, many Dominicans joined the ranks of the unemployed, the destitute, and the hopeless.

The Dominican writers who have achieved visibility in the United States, especially in the 1990s, work against a backdrop of poverty and disempowerment brought about by the economic restructuring this country has experienced over the last three decades. Out of that context comes the work of Junot Díaz, an author who was born in Santo Domingo in 1969. He came to the United States at the age of seven and spent the rest of his childhood and his adolescence in New Jersey, where he attended high school and college. A graduate of Rutgers University, he subsequently applied to Cornell

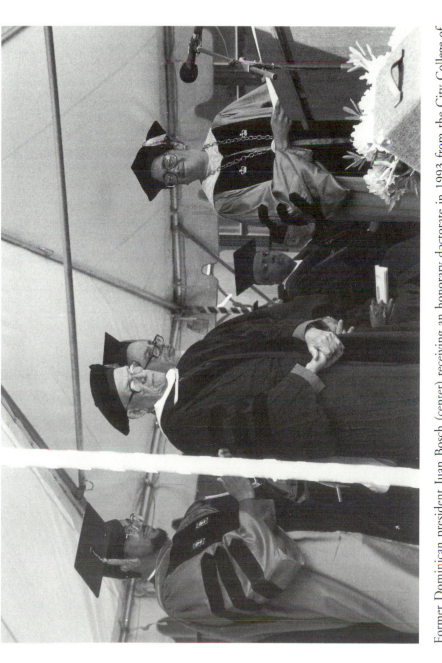

Former Dominican president Juan Bosch (center) receiving an honorary doctorate in 1993 from the City College of New York. Acting President Augusta Souza Kappner is at the podium. Photograph by Philip J. Carvalho courtesy of Dominican Studies Institute archives.

University's prestigious Creative Writing Program. When he left Cornell with an M.F.A. degree in hand, he had already published a short fiction text in the prestigious literary magazine *Story*. Within a month, between the end of 1995 and the beginning of 1996, *The New Yorker* had published two short stories written by him. The January 15, 1996, issue of *Newsweek* carried a story on the "overnight success" of the young Díaz, revealing information about his impressive "six-figure" contract with Riverhead Books, a division of Putnam, for a collection of stories and a novel. Stories by Díaz have earned inclusion in *The Best American Short Stories: 1996* (Houghton Mifflin, 1996) and in the forthcoming *The Best American Short Stories: 1997*. Named a Notable Book of 1996 by the *New York Times Book Review*, the collection of stories *Drown* established Díaz as a vigorous new voice in American fiction.

*Drown*, which appeared in mid-1996, immediately earned the enthusiastic critical reception of reviewers in the *New York Times*, the *Village Voice*, *Publishers Weekly*, and even in fashion and entertainment magazines such as *Elle* and *Mirabella*. The author of *Drown*, who shows a keen intellectual sensibility, delves piercingly into the Dominican chapter of the human experience. His characters, whether living in the Dominican Republic or in their U.S. immigrant locus, confront misery and uprooting. With an exceptional command of words, Díaz communicates emotions and states of mind through concrete images and vivid scenes. The grown-ups in *Drown* vie with unfriendly destinies. Their children, diasporic creatures, have the awe of the American dream thrust upon them by their parents' despair. We come upon the stress inherent in the interaction between the individual and the collective that frames social identity. The imperatives of family, nationality, class, gender, race, community, and sexual proclivity compound the strenuous existence of the characters. A repository of much thought, *Drown* brings to the fore the conflicts, yearnings, and frustrations that have fueled literary texts through the centuries. On the whole, the book presents us with the Dominican experience from the perspective of social marginality and the pain of poverty.

American readers had already been exposed to a literary representation of the experience of the earlier Dominican immigrants, the middle-class families who lived here prior to the great exodus. The poetry and fiction of Julia Alvarez, a writer born in New York to Dominican parents, had already explored their human drama. Born in 1950, Alvarez spent her early childhood in her parents' homeland, where she attended Carol Morgan, an American school, coming back to New York in 1960, when the family felt the need to flee the Trujillo regime. For many years a resident of Middlebury, Vermont, Alvarez is a professor of English at Middlebury College.

Her literary celebrity began in 1984 when Grove Press published her book of poems *Homecoming*, which garnered considerable visibility in the realm of American poetry. Combining narrative with lyrical verse, the volume consists of two parts, one in which the speaker searches for her identity as a woman through an exploration of her mother's teachings about the craft of housekeeping and through an understanding of the worldview informing her mother's culture. The last poem in the section, "Orchids," explores the theme of the woman artist who achieves self-realization through her craft but loses touch with her creativity when marriage occurs. The second section of *Homecoming*, entitled "33," uses the sonnet form to examine the angst of a childless, divorced woman, confronting solitude, sexual desire, the trials of womanhood in an androcentric world, and the awareness of aging with the swift passage of time.

Alvarez has continued writing verse, publishing *The Other Side* in 1995 and *Homecoming: New and Collected Poems* in 1996, both under Penguin Books. The importance attributed to her verse may be illustrated in her selection for inclusion in the exhibition "The Hand of the Poet," a display of "original manuscripts by 100 masters" at the New York Public Library. The second part of the exhibit, which displayed manuscripts of poets from e. e. cummings to Julia Alvarez, remained open to the public from August 16, 1996, through February 15, 1997. Interestingly, her poetry had already received canonical treatment in a 1987 anthology, edited by Robert Bender and Charles Squier, entitled *The Sonnet: An Anthology*, which surveyed practitioners of the sonnet from Sir Thomas Wyatt in the English Renaissance to Julia Alvarez in contemporary American verse.

But it was her fiction that propelled Alvarez to the international plane she now occupies. Her first two books as a storyteller, *How the García Girls Lost Their Accents* (1991) and *In the Time of the Butterflies* (1994), became bestsellers. The third, *¡Yo!*, has earned favorable reviews since it first appeared in 1997. The first was named Notable Book of 1991 by the *New York Times Book Review* and by the American Library Association, and it also received the PEN Oakland/Josephine Miles Award for excellence in literature. The second was nominated for the 1995 National Book Critics Circle Award. Alvarez's work has received national and international prizes and has been translated into other languages. The novel *In the Time of the Butterflies* constitutes her greatest literary achievement thus far. There the author runs aesthetic risks at the level of both style and form, achieving a convincing diction in rendering the lives, passions, and deaths of the Mirabal sisters, three women who made the ultimate sacrifice in challenging the bloodthirsty, misogynist Trujillo dictatorship.

Also among the Dominican writers who use English as their medium of expression is Rhina Espaillat, who comes from the generation prior to that of Alvarez. She was born in La Vega in 1932 and came to this country in 1939. Though she writes primarily in English, she has retained her Spanish and has published poems in newspapers of the Dominican Republic. Espaillat studied at Hunter College of the City University of New York. For her graduate work, she attended Queens College, also in New York City's municipal higher education system. After receiving her MA, she worked as an English teacher in the city's public high schools. Currently, she lives with her husband in Newburyport, Massachusetts. Though not well-known among Dominicans in the United States, probably due to her delaying the publication of her texts until later in life, Espaillat's accomplishments are considerable.

At sixteen, Espaillat became the youngest member ever to have been inducted into the Poetry Society of America. Decades later, the Poetry Society of America would honor her twice, in 1986 and 1989, with its Gustav Davidson Memorial Award. The British magazine *Urbis* also honored her with two awards (Fernández 1994: 79). In 1992 she published her collection of poems *Lapsing to Grace*, which includes her own line drawings as illustrations. The compilations and anthologies that have published Espaillat's poems include *Looking for Home: Women Writing about Exile* (1990), *Sarah's Daughters Sing: A Sampler of Poems by Jewish Women* (1990), *A Formal Feeling Comes: Poems in Form by Contemporary Women* (1994), and *In Other Words: Literature by Latinas of the United States* (1994). The poems of hers gathered in the last of the anthologies listed here evoke memories of childhood and wrestle with distant images of Dominican life. The poet seems interested in conjuring the complex interaction of contemporary poetic diction and traditional forms.

Apart from the literary works written by Dominicans in English, a few important books have entered the U.S. market in translation. Some Dominican literary histories refer in passing to the 1912 novel by Jesusa Alfau y Galván (1895–1943) entitled *Los débiles*, which presumably was rendered into English in New York in 1930, but no information has surfaced regarding its publication. Nearly fifteen years would have to pass for a major publication in English by a Dominican to happen. Pedro Henríquez Ureña's 1940–1941 Charles Elliot Norton Lectures, consisting of an intellectual history and literary survey of Latin America, appeared in book form in 1945 as *Literary Currents of Hispanic America* from Harvard University Press. Years later, UNESCO sponsored *The Sword and the Cross* (1954), an English version of *Enriquillo*, the renowned nineteenth-century novel written by Manuel de

Jesús Galván and translated by Robert Graves. Close to forty years later, the Washington-based small press Azul Editions produced a bilingual collection of verse by the Dominican Republic's poet laureate Pedro Mir entitled *Countersong to Walt Whitman and Other Poems* (1993). That first venture garnered enough success to encourage the publisher to undertake another Dominican project with the 1995 bilingual edition of *Yania Tierra*, an epic poem by Aída Cartagena Portalatín, the dean of Dominican women's writing in the twentieth century. Indiana University Press had published Galván's book through the intervention of UNESCO to serve academic circles. But, Azul Editions' incentive to add Dominican volumes to its titles was clearly the numerical significance of Dominicans in schools, colleges, and universities in the United States today.

The most important recent development in the gradual insertion of Dominican works originally written in Spanish has been the publication of Viriato Sención's *They Forged the Signature of God* (1995) by the Connecticut-based publisher Curbstone Press. The Spanish edition of the novel, *Los que falsificaron la firma de Dios*, had broken all sales records in the country's literary history since it appeared in Santo Domingo in 1992. Dominican readers, including people who had shown no interest in literature before, took to the bookstores in massive numbers. A tale of intrigue, corruption, and deceit set in contemporary times, the novel features characters bearing an unmistakable resemblance to Trujillo, Balaguer, the best-known military chiefs, and Balaguer's influential relatives and associates—the whole gamut of the political scene in the Dominican Republic during the last decades. The novel shows the mendacity of the country's ruling class and government officials. Its indictment proved so effective that President Balaguer himself publicly supported the Minister of Education's decision to revoke the 1993 National Award for Fiction awarded to the work by a panel of experts.

The English version of the novel, translated by Asa Zatz, has received noteworthy reviews in *Publishers Weekly*, the *Washington Post Book World*, *Choice*, and the *Latino Review of Books*, among others. During the 1996 presidential election in the Dominican Republic, the *New York Times* quoted various fragments from *They Forged the Signature of God* to illustrate the behavior of some of the contenders in the political contest. Sención wrote the novel in the South Bronx, in New York, where he had lived for nearly fifteen years. Though the book deals with political situations of the homeland, its scathing indictment of the Dominican power structure reflects a diaspora perspective that inside the country would be inconceivable. It was arguably the distance from the native land that sharpened the author's memory and activated his critical sense. *They Forged the Signature of God* draws much of its artistic tension from the author's passionate recall of his homeland's social and political reality. At one point, we hear the character Arturo musing about his uncle Julio's New York stories:

You stay in your apartment for months while it's cold or snowing outside. Your neighbors are like ghosts, always in a hurry, who don't even say hello to you. You ride in the subway, going and coming, and you have a crowd of people for company who are either hostile, alienated, or asleep. And where are you going? Into the void. (Sención 1995: 100–101)

Uncle Julio's testimony evokes a stage in an immigrant group's process of adaptation to a host country that is marked by existential angst, psychological distance from one's immediate surroundings, and a deep sense of nostalgia and solitude, corresponding to Sención's state of mind during the latter half of the 1980s when acute childhood memories and a sharp scrutiny of contemporary Dominican politics were united in his first novel. This book constitutes an important stage in the Dominican community's coping with the political events that caused its migration.

   The gradual increase in visibility of Dominican letters in the United States, by means of translation into English of important Dominican works or the rise of a few Anglophone Dominican writers, has been assisted, in part, by an emerging cadre of academics committed to the cause of disseminating knowledge about the Dominican experience. In April 1986, Carlos Rodríguez Matos, of the Romance Languages Department at Seton Hall, organized, in collaboration with Rutgers University, a three-day scholarly event called "First Multidisciplinary Conference on Dominican Republic," which brought together many Dominicanists from American and Dominican universities. In 1988 the prestigious literary journal *Revista Iberoamericana*, edited by a distinguished Hispanist, the late Alfredo A. Roggiano of the University of Pittsburgh, dedicated a whole issue to Dominican literature (vol. 54, no. 142). The issue was prepared by Rei Berroa, a Dominican-born Spanish literature scholar from George Mason University.

   Following those two milestones, the most important efforts of dissemination of knowledge about Dominican cultural products have been championed by New York–based Dominican scholars. Daisy Cocco de Filippis, a literary scholar and translator at York College, of the City University of New York, has spearheaded many pioneering ventures. She has compiled two invaluable anthologies of the writings of Dominican women from colonial times to the present—one covers verse and the other, prose fiction. The two

Dominican poet laureate Pedro Mir (center) with Professor Ana María Hernández (left) and former WNJU-TV newscaster Mari Santana, at a cultural function in Washington Heights. © Eduardo Hoepelman, courtesy of Dominican Studies Institute archives.

compilations bring to the fore the need to reconfigure the chronicle of Dominican literary history from the point of view of gender. She has also co-edited two bilingual collections of the writings of Dominicans in the United States: one focuses on poetry, *Poems of Exile and Other Concerns* (1988), and the other on fiction, *Stories of Washington Heights and Other Corners of the World* (1994). She has also compiled *Tertuliando/Hanging Out* (1997), a gathering of poetry, short fiction, and essays written by Dominican and other Latina women whose periodic readings she had coordinated. De Filippis spearheaded the Dominican Studies Association as founding president in the mid-1990s, just as sociologist Ramona Hernández, cochair with higher education administrator Ana García Reyes of the Council of Dominican Educators, had led the effort to create the City University's Dominican Studies Institute.

However, despite the notable gains summarized here, Dominican literature in the United States continues to be a marginal cultural expression. The majority of Dominican authors write predominantly in Spanish for the virtually exclusive consumption of small literary circles in Dominican neighborhoods. These literary artists have very few publication opportunities. Normally, they have to finance, supervise production, and distribute their own books. They have hardly any chance of becoming included in mainstream literary markets or at least of attaining a level of prestige outside of their immigrant enclaves. In other words, Dominican writing remains generally relegated to what has been called "the periphery of the margins" (Torres-Saillant 1991). Yet, one cannot help but have faith in the persistence, tenacity, and indomitability of Dominican writers as they continue to publish against all odds. A mere listing of the authors who in the last decade have committed their poems, novels, and short fiction to print illustrates their dynamism: Carlos Rodríguez, Marianela Medrano, Alexis Gómez Rosa, Franklin Gutiérrez, Miriam Ventura, León Félix Batista, Rei Berroa, Juan Rivero, José Carvajal, Tomás Modesto Galán, Julio Alvarado, Norberto James Rawlings, Juan Torres, Teonilda Madera, Diógenes Abréu, Irene Santos, Josefina Báez, Félix Darío Mendoza, Juan Matos, José Segura, Ynoemia Villar, and Dagoberto López, to name only the most active. Whether or not their works prove enduring, the community will owe them appreciation for assuming the task of bearing witness to the inexorably traumatic immigrant experience of their people.

## VISUAL ARTS

The presence of Dominicans in painting, sculpture, graphic design, and mixed media in the United States defies coherent descriptions. Since Dominican artists have traveled to North America for different reasons, at different times, and under different circumstances, an overview of their work here can follow no easy pattern. Historically, the contact of Dominicans with the art world in this country dates back at least to 1922, when Celeste Woss y Gil, "the grand dame of Dominican modernist painting," began the first of two sojourns in New York. By the end of her second stay in the city in 1931, Woss y Gil had spent five years in New York, studying at the prestigious Art Student League and absorbing the aesthetic currents then transforming the plastic arts in the cultural capitals of the West (Pellegrini 1996b: 23). The daughter of former President Alejandro Woss y Gil, who had ruled the Dominican Republic from 1885 to 1887, she lived in France, Cuba, and the United States during her father's exile. She possessed a privileged social rank that permitted her to pursue the highest artistic education in each of the countries where she lived.

New York's Art Student League has continued to be a desirable school for aspiring artists from the Dominican Republic to pursue their training. A contemporary painter, Alberto Bass, who was born in Santo Domingo in 1949, came to study in that school in 1967. As we gather from the biographical information printed in *Historia y bachata: Colonización y neocolonización*, a catalogue/lecture he published in Santo Domingo in 1993, during his years in New York, Bass established contact with the working-class Dominican community that already had emerged in Washington Heights. He lectured at the community organization Club Orlando Martínez in northern Manhattan, and, back in Santo Domingo, in 1981 he launched an exhibit entitled "La vida del dominicano en Nueva York" (The Life of Dominicans in New York). Bass is separated from Woss y Gil by a vast difference of class, generation, and circumstances, which probably explains his rapport with the community. Like her, he returned to practice his art in the native land.

Among those who stayed in the United States, the most senior are Tito Enrique Cánepa, born in San Pedro de Macorís in 1916, and Darío Suro, who was born in La Vega in 1917 and died in 1997. Cánepa fled the Trujillo dictatorship in his native land in 1935. "After two years in Puerto Rico, he moved to New York where he worked in the Sisqueiros Workshop and studied art and composition in WPA art schools" (Pellegrini 1996b: 114). The WPA art projects in the 1930s stimulated Cánepa, and the cultural dynamism of the city fueled his work with rich possibilities for expression. He has exhibited work in New York at least since 1938. One wonders, therefore, about the outright omission of his name from the survey *The Latin American Spirit: Art and Artists in the United States, 1920–1970*, a retrospective overview published in 1988 based on an exhibition sponsored by the Bronx Museum of the Arts which failed to include one single Dominican among the 165 artists considered. At any rate, though reflecting a wide range of aesthetic lessons drawn from diverse international currents and retaining a thematic interest in episodes of Dominican history, Cánepa's artistic production emanates from his nearly six decades of living in the United States.

Suro, on the other hand, spent time in Mexico, where he studied under Diego Rivera and other master muralists. He came to the United States only after he had attained recognition in the Dominican Republic as a first-rate painter. He traveled widely and received distinctions at home and abroad. In 1962 he had a one-man exhibition at the Poindexter Gallery in New York. For many years he lived in Washington, D.C., where he continued to paint vigorously and to write art criticism while serving in the Dominican embassy as a cultural attaché until his death. Although Suro was far from his country, his work continued to reflect a concern with the uniqueness of Dominican culture, as art historian Elena Pellegrini has noted (1996b: 28). Next among the recognized Dominican masters is Clara Ledesma, who was born in Santiago in 1924. She began exhibiting as a solo artist in 1952 and has achieved much international recognition, and today her work forms part of the permanent exhibit of the major museums in her country. Art historian Jeannette Miller says that Ledesma "resided a long time in New York, where she held exhibits and maintained her own art gallery," after which she moved to Santo Domingo (Miller 1984: 122). For the last decade, Ledesma has resettled in New York, where she lives and works largely unknown to the Dominican community, which has become the second largest immigrant component of the city's population. The late Eligio Pichardo (1929–1984), who for seventeen years lived in New York, where he had solo shows in several private galleries, has had his work included in the collection of the Metropolitan Museum of Art (Pellegrini 1996b: 118).

Without a doubt, however, the 1980s marked a turning point for Dominican artists, who began to take major strides toward visibility in this country. Early in that decade, several expatriate Dominican painters and sculptors formed a loose association known as the Dominican Visual Artists of New York (DVANY) "with the goal of presenting the works of its members to an American public that knew almost nothing about these artists or their Dominican heritage" (Kaplan 1996: 14–15). At that time, the group included Bismarck Victoria, Freddy Rodríguez, Eligio Reynoso, Magno Laracuente, and Tito Cánepa, painters who, for the most part, felt dissatisfied with the lack of venues for their work. The gallery establishment did not seem interested enough in displaying their work. In 1984 the members of DVANY launched a collective exhibit with considerable success at the gallery of the Department of Cultural Affairs of the City of New York on Columbus Circle in midtown Manhattan. The divergent styles and diversity of expressions and forms surprised many who had not expected such richness (1996: 14–15). The following year, in November 1995, Gulf and Western "turned over the lobby of its 59th Street headquarters" to an exhibition, the first ever in that space, by the New York–based Dominican sculptor Victoria, one of the members of DVANY (15).

Stephen D. Kaplan, himself a founding member of DVANY and the rector of the Altos de Chavón/The School of Design in La Romana, Dominican Republic, the alma mater of many of the young Dominican artists currently in the United States, believes that the group drew extensively on "the vast new art stream flooding the international media" as well as the dynamism of life in New York (Kaplan 1996: 15). But, most important, the "burgeoning Dominican community in Manhattan" offered these artists a cultural framework and an emotional context that often proved profitable. One remarkable case of the cross-fertilization of the artist with the community is that of Carlos Reynoso. A 1996 recipient of the prestigious Artist's Projects grant awarded by the National Endowment for the Arts, the Rockefeller Foundation, and the Andy Warhol Foundation for the Visual Arts, Reynoso has shunned the gallery circuit, preferring "instead the creation of pieces that are anonymous and ephemeral—often done in conjunction with Dominican students in Washington Heights, whom he voluntarily teaches," according to Alanna Lockward in her words of presentation of the artist for a brochure describing his exhibit in the Santo Domingo Museum Casa de Bastidas on August 5, 1996.

On the whole, the Dominican art scene in the United States is probably best summarized by several important exhibits that have been presented in New York since 1992. The first, entitled "Dominicaras Dominicosas," an exhibition of photography, painting, and utilitarian sculpture seeking to document and celebrate Dominican migration, was shown at the Hostos Art Gallery from April 14 to May 29, 1992, under the curatorship of Josefina Báez. The exhibit featured the work of Onorío Pérez, Richard Powel, Radhames Morales, Scherezade García Vázquez, and Pilar Gonzales. The second, entitled "500 Yolas," displayed paintings, sculptures, and drawings by New York–based Dominican artists on topics inspired by the quincentenary of the conquest of the Americas. Held from November 4, 1992, through January

15, 1993, at the Hostos Art Gallery in the Bronx, the exhibit featured works by Scherezade García, Danilo González, Hochi Asiático, Moses Rios, and Germán Pérez, all very successful young artists. The third, entitled "Modern and Contemporary Art of the Dominican Republic," opened first in New York at the contiguous galleries of the main sponsoring institutions, the Americas Society and The Spanish Institute, from June 14 to August 4, 1996, and then at the Bass Museum of Art in Miami, Florida, from October 3 to December 1, 1996. Although this exhibit focused primarily on surveying the artistic production of the Dominican Republic, it did include four U.S.-based names in the selection of the thirty-two artists that made up the show: Cánepa, Rodríguez, Suro, and Victoria. The fourth exhibit, held at INTAR Latin American Gallery in Manhattan, was called "Art in Transit: A Dominican Experience:" Part One, featuring the work of Hochi Asiático, Raquel Paiewonsky, Julia Santos Solomon, and Darío Suro, was open from September 26 to October 26, 1996. Part Two, presenting work by Crucelyn Ferreira, Freddy Rodríguez, Etienne H. Stanley, and Julio Valdez, was open from November 4 to November 30, 1996. Unlike previous efforts, this art show, conceived originally by Pellegrini when she directed the Gallery at INTAR, specifically concentrated on "Dominican artists currently living in the United States," in order to give an idea of how contemporary Dominican artists have developed outside of their native country (Casares 1996: 9). Since residence in the United States at the time of the exhibit was the only common factor that linked the artists, apart, of course, from the curators' aesthetic considerations about the quality of the pieces displayed, the show permitted considerable disparity in the nature of the artists' relationship with American society. The duration of their stay in this country, for instance, ranged from five years, in the cases of Stanley and Valdez, to nearly three decades in the case of Solomon.

Neither this exhibit nor any other of the art shows mentioned in this overview exhaust the wide range of artistic talent and activity produced by Dominican immigrants in the United States. For instance, thirty-five-year-old Magno Laracuente, who has lived in New York since 1979 and was part of the original DVANY group in 1984, did not appear in any of the exhibits listed above despite his relative success both in the Dominican Republic and in the United States. Also absent was painter Gerardo Phillips, a Dominican residing in New York, who has been influenced by Wildredo Lam and Marc Chagall, as he acknowledges in the book *Caribbean Visions*, an overview of contemporary Caribbean painters and sculptors that includes work of his (Phillips 1995: 124). There are also lesser known Dominican artists of the diaspora, including Diógenes Abréu, who has participated in exhibitions in

New York and Tokyo galleries. Abréu, unlike many of the artists surveyed herein, began to paint in New York, where he, by virtue of his own working-class origin, has shared the immigrant experience of his people on a day-to-day basis in marginal social settings such as the Dominican neighborhood of Washington Heights.

Ironically, the visual artists who are most closely and painfully connected with the plight of the Dominican community are the practitioners of memorial art, an offspring of the graffiti movement that emerged in the 1980s (Camacho 1996: 126–27). Jhovanny Camacho, former curator of the Museum of Contemporary Hispanic Art in New York City, speaks of memorial art as "an underground" expression whereby "a community or elements within it" seek "to perpetuate the remembrance of members gone before their time." While the street murals normally depict the plight of the deviant, primarily young men who have "fallen in territorial drug wars," they also include some who have died of other causes (1996: 127). The majority of the Dominican youngsters honored with memorials are unknown to a large sector of the community where the work is exhibited. According to Camacho, "Anonymity is one of the most interesting facts in Dominican memorial art. Both the artist and the honored subject remain anonymous" (133–34). Their anonymity, plus their thematic engagement with death and "shattered dreams," painfully reflect the harshness of the immigrant experience for many Dominicans in the United States.

## PERFORMING ARTS

With the death on April 6, 1996, of Ilka Tanya Payán, the Dominican community in the United States lost one of its very few prominent theater personalities. Born in Santo Domingo in 1943, Payán came to North America in 1956. An attorney with an immigration law practice since 1984, having received her Juris Doctor degree four years earlier, she wrote a column on immigration issues for the New York Hispanic newspaper *El Diario/La Prensa* and for the New York edition of the Dominican daily *El Nacional.* Payán began acting in 1969, performing mostly in Spanish-language theaters in New York City, but her dramatic work also took her to Spain, Puerto Rico, and the Dominican Republic. She played a leading role in *Angélica, mi vida*, the first Spanish-language soap opera to air nationally in the United States, broadcast via Telemundo, the Spanish-speaking television network. Payán also played parts in some Anglophone American film and television productions, most notably in HBO's *Florida Straits*, in which she costarred with the late Raul Julia.

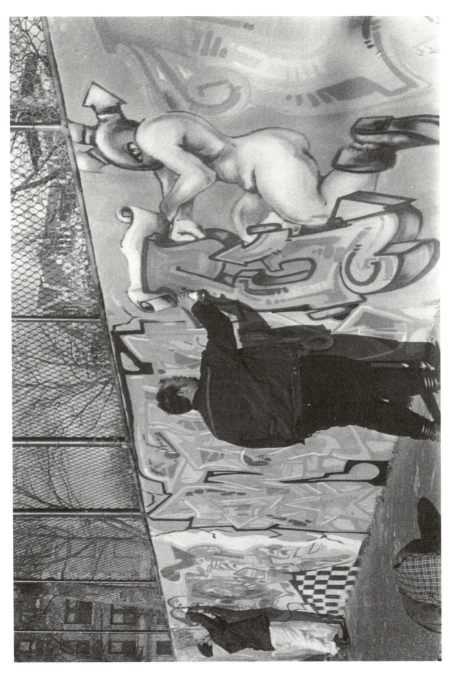

Street muralists at work in a schoolyard in northern Manhattan. © Josefina Báez.

Payán became a lawyer because she was afraid she would not be able to support herself solely on her acting career, but her legal services "drew her increasingly into public affairs" (Navarro 1993; Thomas, Jr. 1996). A volunteer with many direct service community organizations, such as Catholic Charities and the Center for Immigrants, she was associated with the Gay Men's Health Crisis since 1984, first as a volunteer and subsequently as supervisor of the organization's Legal Services Department. Linking her interest in legal affairs with her love of the theater, she often donated her work as a counsel for theater groups like the Actor's Fund and various cultural institutions such as the Association of Hispanic Arts.

Payán had become so prominent in the defense of human rights for immigrants and for people with HIV in Hispanic political and civic circles that in 1992 Mayor David N. Dinkins appointed her to the City of New York's Commission on Human Rights. Ironically, though she had enjoyed a successful career as an actress, within the relative marginality of the Latino theater in the Northeast, it was really her startling announcement that she had contracted the HIV virus that propelled her to a broad national stage. Her declaration at a press conference on October 14, 1993, was saluted the following day by *El Diario/La Prensa* (October 15, 1993) with front-page coverage, a three-page feature article, and an editorial. The paper celebrated Payán for giving "us all a lesson in personal courage, and we fully agree with her hopes that her confession will serve to educate and dissipate the ignorance that often surrounds this disease, especially in the Latino community." She subsequently became the object of much coverage by the *New York Times, Time* magazine, the major television networks, and the media in general. She received multiple invitations to appear at AIDS conferences and events, and she garnered the spotlight on December 1, 1993, during a United Nations forum on World AIDS.

After her death, Payán elicited much homage and many tributes, including a lengthy obituary article in the *New York Times* (April 8, 1996). There was something theatrical, in the best possible sense, about the way Payán conducted herself during the last three years of her life. Her public confession and its consequences became her most trying performance. Showing that she had the necessary mettle, she confronted the drama of human existence with bold determination to put an end to thirteen years of fearful silence after she became infected. Some of her words from the statement before the press on October 14, 1993, ring clear with a profound understanding of personal tragedy and public responsibility:

My family in the Dominican Republic fears reprisals. Yet, before their fear as people without HIV, is my fear living with it. I have had to choose not to be silent and frightened anymore. If I continue to do this, it will mean that I agree with the discrimination. Having to keep this secret is collaborating with the intolerable social abnormality of treating a health problem as a moral and political issue (Press release, October 14, 1993).

With her impressive grand finale, Payán achieved a visibility comparable to that of only one other Dominican compatriot, the memorable María Montez.

Other than the theater and film personalities already cited, only actor Mateo Gómez among Dominicans in the United States is known to have succeeded at building a stable acting career on the broader commercial stage, beyond the narrow confines of community productions in the Latino theater. Gómez has had many accomplishments in the theater, in television, and in film. He played an important part in a Broadway production of Tennessee Williams' *A Streetcar Named Desire*, and he has done numerous spots for television advertising. He also costarred with Chuck Norris in the movie *Delta Force II*. Another notable success story was that of Dominican actor and director Rolando Barrera, whose group Futurismo succeeded in the 1940s in staging four productions a year of Spanish versions of European plays at the Master's Auditorium (Kanellos 1994: 473). The careers of these artists shed light only on the challenges of individual Dominicans determined to pursue their goals and aspirations as actors and their possibility to cross over to the mainstream of the industry. None of the cases mentioned, however, can suggest a strong Dominican theater tradition in the making to match the rise of the Dominican immigrant settlements that have spread throughout the United States.

The most extraordinary cases aside, Dominican actors and playwrights cannot boast of a stage of their own with loyal audiences that serve as interlocutors to their work. For the most part, they must hire their talent out to theater groups and companies that cater generally to Latinos or specifically to those Hispanic subgroups that have lived a longer time in the United States, such as Cubans and Puerto Ricans, the dominant Latino communities in the Northeast. In New York, for instance, Dominican theatrical talent has often found a place in Repertorio Español, Puerto Rican Travelling Theater, Hostos Center for the Arts and Culture, Pregones Theater, Teatro Cuatro, La Tea Theater, Duo Theater, and Thalia Theater, to name a few of the best known. The explanation for the absence of specifically Dominican venues for talented actors and playwrights lies in the precarious socioeconomic conditions of the community. Theaters require sizable monetary investments, spacious locales, opportunities for the training and technical advancement of actors and playwrights, and audiences that have the interest and the funds

The late Ilka Tanya Payán reciting at New York's United Palace Theater before a large Dominican audience. © Eduardo Hoepelman, courtesy of Dominican Studies Institute archives.

to keep productions alive. A welcome development, though, is the effort of long-established companies like Repertorio Español to attract Dominican audiences by importing from the Dominican Republic well-known playwrights such as Franklin Domínguez and companies such as Teatro Gayumba. Perhaps that outreach effort will foment audience development, which may eventually have positive repercussions for U.S.-based Dominican theaters.

The most promising sign of a possible bright future for a Dominican theater in the United States lies in efforts of the kind championed by Latinarte, whose artistic director, the actress, dancer, author, and teacher Josefina Báez, upholds an equal commitment to technical accomplishment, thematic relevancy, and audience development. Born in La Romana in 1960, Báez arrived in the United States in 1972. After her secondary education in New York City's public school system, she pursued training in dance, studying classical dance for eight years at the American Dance School, modern and jazz dance for four years at the New York Dance Troupe, and Oriental and Indian dance under recognized masters in New Delhi and New York. Her training in drama began formally with her seven years under Flora Lauten of the Buendía Theater Group in Cuba, which continued until the latter half of the 1990s, when she resumed the exploration of "theatrical biomechanics," the technique developed by Russian master Gennady Bogdanov, a protegé of the late Nikolai Kustov as well as an actor and teacher in Meyerhold's famous company. In addition to her in-depth study of acting and dance techniques, Báez attended the Latino Playwright Lab at the Public Theater in New York City, as a result of which she wrote *It's a New York Thang; You Will Understand*, a play first presented in a staged reading at the Public Theater in 1994.

Professionally, Báez has traveled widely to perform both as a dancer and as an actress. Rio de Janerio's Municipal Ballet hired her as a *balletista* during four consecutive fall seasons from 1980 through 1984. An engagement with the International Theater Institute workshop took her to Cuba in 1983. In 1986 she appeared as a guest performer in major festivals held in Mexico and France. She worked with distinction in Helsinski, Finland, in 1989, and returned to Cuba to honor a commitment with the Latin American and Caribbean Theater School in 1994. In early 1997 she performed in Russia, upon the invitation of Bogdanov, as well as in Spain. Complementing her professional work as a performer, Báez devotes considerable time to teaching drama and creative writing primarily to children and adolescents through a program jointly sponsored by Teachers and Writers Artsconnection and Latinarte. Since 1984, when that initiative began, Báez has taught in virtually every New York City public school that has a significant Dominican student population, from kindergarten through the senior year of high school.

Whether in the classroom or on the stage, the creed informing Báez's work invariably gives priority to artistic experimentation, audience development, and authentic representation. When approaching the human experience, she focuses especially on the life of her people as a cultural, political, and linguistic minority in the United States. The titles of the dramatic pieces Báez has authored, "performance texts" as she prefers to call them, from *Negritud dominicana* (Dominican blackness, 1986) to *In Dominicanish* (1996), as well as her poems "I am Dominican but," published in *Forward Motion* (summer 1996), and "Migration," which appeared in *Scholastic Anthology of Caribbean Women Writers* (1992), indicate an unswerving dedication to the search for meaning in the midst of the potential disorientation of a diasporic existence. Central to the artistic creed that governs Latinarte's aesthetic agenda is the determination to tackle the challenges and possibilities of Dominicans in the United States through an experimental theatrical expression that avoids linearity both of text and dramaturgy. "Though we respect them greatly," Báez has said, "we do not deal with the works of the classics, be it Shakespeare or García Lorca. Nor do we touch the known masters of Latin American theater. We only stage plays that emerge from the experience of the diaspora by playwrights who have lived that experience" (personal interview with author).

A black woman whose ancestral line links her directly to the African-descended sugarcane workers of the *bateyes* of La Romana, Báez draws on the mental transformations set in motion by migration to peruse many of the social, political, and cultural myths of the Dominican Republic. The linguistic, racial, religious, and ethnic diversity of New York fuels the discourse of her performance texts, which ingeniously indict the negrophobia, conservatism, misogyny, homophobia, Eurocentrism, and upper-class bias that characterize official Dominican discourse as reflected in the pronouncements of Catholic Church leaders, mainstream politicians, and state-funded intellectuals in the sending society. At the same time, she celebrates the cultural hybridity that diaspora Dominicans normally develop while poking fun at the xenophobic prejudice that often causes others in the larger American society to raise a disapproving eyebrow in the face of Dominican difference.

One of Latinarte's most successful recent productions, *Lo mío es mío* (What's mine is mine, 1994), one of the many results of the fruitful collaboration of Báez with playwright and director Claudio Mir, tells the story of the Dominican people, from life in the home country through the plight of

Josefina Báez, publicity photo. Photograph by M. Hanney © Josefina Báez.

the diaspora, by means of various renderings of well-known children's games. The play draws on kathak, an Indian dance, as well as on traditional Dominican songs and carnival traditions to scrutinize political leaders and their harmful legacy to the Dominican people, and closes with the anxieties that emanate from the trials of immigration to the United States. An aesthetically successful undertaking, *Lo mío es mío*, like many of Latinarte's dramatic ventures, relies on a minimal number of highly versatile actors, sparse but well-aimed lighting, and a stage with scanty decorations or props. The streamlined format, which recalls the economy of the early Athenian tragic stage, makes for relatively inexpensive productions that can without undue difficulty move from one site to another and adjust to spaces not necessarily conceived for theatrical performance. Therein lies the invaluable model rehearsed by Latinarte. With the leadership of Báez and her dedication to artistic enhancement through the sharpening of technical resources, Latinarte has shown the possibility of producing work that is creative in form and content even in an immigrant community that has not yet reached the state of maturity and social sophistication required for the establishment of expensive and permanent theatrical ventures with large, conscientious audiences to support them.

## POPULAR MUSIC

The most salient cultural presence of Dominicans in the United States has occurred in the realm of popular music with the increasing acceptance of merengue, the best-known Dominican dance music, in Latino entertainment circles during the 1980s and 1990s. Merengue first traveled to North America in the 1920s, when groups such as Trio Borinquen, alternately called Trio Quisqueya, fulfilled recording contracts with Columbia Records in New York (Del Castillo and García Arévalo 1988: 45). In 1928 RCA Victor's International Orchestra marketed tropical rhythms that included three merengues. The following year and thenceforward for two decades, Dominican artists went to the company's New York studio for all recording work (Pacini Hernández 1995: 49). In 1940 the classical music conductor Leopold Stokowski, then on a world tour, visited the Dominican Republic with his orchestra aboard the transatlantic ship *Argentina*, which was equipped with a small recording studio. Stokowski invited the Dominican musician Luis Alberti and his orchestra to come on board for a recording session, and the result was the production of twenty numbers that would subsequently open the doors of Columbia Records to Dominican artists (Del Castillo and García Arévalo 1988: 47).

During the 1950s, Angel Victoria, leading the ensemble Conjunto Típico Quisqueyano, recorded many popular numbers for Ansonia Records in New York, and Napoleón Zayas, at the head of the group Napoleón and his Boys, performed at many of New York's most popular entertainment sites, including the Alhambra, the Savoy Ballroom, and the Cotton Club (Del Castillo García Arévalo 1988: 47). Since the 1930s

Niño Durán had formed his own orchestra, Enrique Durán and his Saint Domingo Serenaders, that played at the Savoy Ballroom, located on a First Avenue building

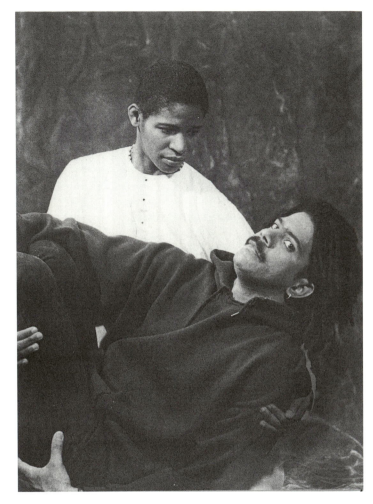

Promotional photo of Josefina Báez and Claudio Mir in *Lo mio es mio*. Photograph by Julio Nazario © Claudio Mir/Latinarte.

that took the whole block. This ballroom accommodated as many as 5,000 dancers, and it attracted a multiracial crowd that made it one of the most democratic entertainment locales in New York and possibly even in the United States. (Roberts Hernández 1986: 70)

Originally hired for two months, Durán's orchestra played there for six years due to his popularity.

By the same token, the venerated baritone Eduardo Brito, whose prodigious voice became legendary in Dominican cultural history, completed two extended professional seasons in this country. During a first tour, from 1929 to 1932, he came to honor an RCA Victor recording contract and received numerous additional invitations to sing in restaurants, theaters, halls, and radio stations. Brito and his wife, Elena, also a singer and dancer who performed with him, came back to North America in 1938. Without the same level of success of his earlier sojourn, they nonetheless performed at the Paramount, Roxy, Radio City, and Hispano theaters, all in New York City, and sang as special guests at the inauguration of the Hispanic Cabaret El Bongó on April 21, 1938 (Roberts Hernández 1986: 125). These musicians, along with others like singer Negrito Chapuseaux, pianist Simó Damirón, band leader Billo Frómeta, and vocalist Alberto Beltrán, in addition to the Trujillo regime's concerted efforts to export a particular brand of merengue, share the credit for introducing Dominican popular music to the United States and Europe in the first half of the twentieth century.

With the advent of their great exodus to the United States, the musical forms of Dominicans gained increasing visibility in North America. By the 1970s merengue had grown so much in popularity that it was seen as a rival of salsa. Salsa, however, was more firmly grounded in Latin New York:

Salsa was an unmistakable product of the modern Pan-Caribbean experience: salsa musicians were mostly Puerto Rican, its rhythms were principally Cuban, and its social context was primarily the Latin barrios of New York City. Emerging in the mid-to-late 1960s, salsa was aggressively promoted all over Latin America by the New York–based Fania record company. (Pacini Hernández 1995: 107)

The role of Dominican Johnny Pacheco as one of the pillars of the early development of salsa suggests that "Dominicans could claim at least some measure of paternity for salsa" (1995: 107). Despite the overwhelming popularity of salsa, however, Dominican merengue bands continued to thrive. Such New York–based groups as Dominica and Primitivo Santos y su Combo remained in demand in Hispanic night clubs throughout the 1970s. By the mid-1980s, merengue was the most requested Caribbean music in the United States. Not only did it seem to have "besieged" salsa, but its success inspired even non-Dominicans to form merengue bands in the mainland United States and Puerto Rico (Austerlitz 1997: 127–28).

One of the clearest milestones in the development of Dominican music outside of the Dominican Republic was the rise of the group Milly, Jocelyn y Los Vecinos in the 1980s. Made up of four siblings—two brothers as musicians and Milly and her sister Jocelyn as vocalists—the group originated in New York. The involvement of relatives to set up the venture of a musical organization highlights the role of the family as the core of entrepreneurial activity for many Dominican immigrants in the United States. By the same token, the leadership of Milly and Jocelyn as vibrant vocalists accentuates the position of women in the artistic undertakings of the Dominican community, which comes as no surprise given the numerical superiority of women over men in the migratory movement. Milly is reported to be "the first woman to sing down-home merengue commercially" (Hanley 1991: 44). Many of the songs made popular by Milly and Jocelyn y Los Vecinos deal with issues related to the tensions and transformations emanating from the experience of immigration (Del Castillo and García Arévalo 1988: 90). Milly's songs had a special appeal to women. A commentator who attended her concerts during her tour in Santo Domingo noted that "it's the women who push closest to Milly, making a kind of chorus in front of the band . . . it's mostly about ladies leaving their *machista* men that Milly sings" (Hanley 1991: 44). Another observer of the Latin music scene has noted the extent to which Milly opened doors for women, even back in the home country where the success of the all-female band Las Chicas del Can and the presence of women as lead singers in mixed bands suggest that merengue now presents real opportunities for women (Holston 1990: 54). Following in the wake of Milly's success, a number of New York–based Dominican music bands have since then proliferated on the show business market. The New York Band, La Gran Manzana, Oro Sólido, and La Banda Loca are among them.

Another Dominican rhythm that has successfully vied for space in the popular music market of New York's entertainment industry is *bachata*, which was, until recently, "a musical pariah" in the Dominican Republic due to its link with the popular classes: "Since its emergence in the early 1960s, bachata, closely associated with poor rural migrants residing in urban shanty towns, was considered too crude, too vulgar, and too musically rustic to be allowed entrance into the mainstream musical landscape." Despite its popularity and huge sales, "no bachata record ever appeared on a published hit parade list, received airplay on FM radio stations in the country's capital, Santo Domingo, or were [*sic*] sold in the principal record stores" (Pacini Hernández 1995: 1). With the flow of Dominicans to the United States, cities with large Latino populations became target markets for *bachata* practitioners, such as Tony Santos and Blas Durán, according to Dominican music historian Arístides Incháustegui (1995: 245). Apparently, the vast New York market allowed them a freedom they had not enjoyed back home. Their songs became ever more risky, making the play with double entendre more explicit than it had been before (1995: 245).

Since 1991, the year when Juan Luis Guerra and his 4:40 Group released a recording entitled "Bachata Rosa," which achieved immediate worldwide success, *bachata* has ceased to suffer rejection by middle-class Dominican society. One of the most successful in the recent history of Latin music, "Bachata Rosa" sold over 3.5 million copies internationally and won a Grammy award in the Latin Tropical category in 1992 (Pacini Hernández 1995: 2). Guerra's middle-class origins would not have naturally inclined him toward a socially stigmatized musical form such as *bachata*. The contact with the United States, where he came to receive advanced musical training at Boston's Berklee College of Music, may have provoked his exploration of the music of the lower classes. North American artists have long delved into the rhythmic productions of marginal sectors of society. Witness the cases of jazz, rhythm and blues, and most recently rap. That tradition may have encouraged Guerra, away from the elite cultural circles of Santo Domingo, to touch base with a musical form associated with people at the lower ranks of Dominican society. Also although he returned to Santo Domingo soon after finishing his studies, he retained an interest in the fortunes of the Dominican community in North America, as is reflected in the lyrics of many of his songs such as "Visa para un sueño" (Visa for a Dream).

Two other avant-garde artists, Luis Díaz, a composer, performer, and band leader who was probably the first of the legitimate Dominican musicians to experiment with *bachata*, and Michael Camilo, who has attained distinction as a pianist and jazz band leader, both live in New York. Díaz has remained active playing primarily at middle-to high-brow Latino cultural centers. In the fall of 1996 Camilo could be seen regularly on Channel 41-TV as part of the station's promotional campaign. Other than Camilo and Guerra, few Dominican performers have crossed over to mainstream American audiences. On the whole, their haven remains limited to Hispanic television and radio, the night club entertainment scene, and cable television channels, especially public access ones. Occasionally, though, one may hear a Dominican tune being used as background music or a theme for a program on Fox Television Network, suggesting the possibility that Dominican popular music may in the years to come gain acceptance in the entertainment industry of the larger society, beyond the confines of the Hispanic or Caribbean community. The trend of Dominicans of the next generation will probably not continue to be that of replicating the established forms of music from the home country, be it *bachata* or merengue. Rather, it will be the creation of alternative forms, combining the rhythms of the native land with those found in the host country just as the leaders of Proyecto Uno have done. Made up of Dominican and other Latino young men, slightly reminiscent of The Jackson 5 or a dark-skinned version of Menudo, Proyecto Uno has succeeded in creating an aesthetic of its own by drawing from Dominican and Latin sounds and mixing them with elements of rap, house, and other musical modalities from hip-hop urban culture in the United States. The successful experiments of Proyecto Uno may be prognosticating a bright future for Dominican popular music in the United States.

## FAITH AND FOOD

Neighborhoods populated by significant numbers of Dominicans normally exhibit the cultural accent of the community in a strikingly visual way. Contributing to the visual aspect of the Dominican presence is a proliferation of stores that emulate the ways of the tropics by extending their commercial space onto the sidewalk. The unemployed or underemployed often resort to survival strategies replicated from the homeland, namely the creation of improvised business structures. A woman may operate a restaurant out of a basement or a clothing store out of a small apartment. A man may fry *empanadas* or *pastelitos* at his makeshift ambulatory kitchen on a street corner. Dominicans do much outside. Community members, especially the males, gather at the bodegas or on open spaces to chat about current events. Beside the inevitable coming and going of parents walking their children to and from school, there is also the mobility of employees who have jobs outside of the neighborhood. On the whole, the community may appear to outsiders to be replete with people moving hither and thither.

Two factors, faith and food, stand out among those responsible for the impression of constant movement and colorfulness in Dominican neighborhoods. Starting with food, one cannot miss the way in which grocery stores mark neighborhoods with a distinguishing cultural seal. Displayed outside many bodegas, the wide variety of tropical staples, from brownish cassava, to green plantain, to purple-skinned eggplant, generates much visual richness. Small carts selling tropical ice cones or peeled oranges appear in the summer. Their counterparts in the winter dispense hot sweet drinks such as *habichuelas con dulce* or soups. Similarly, restaurants and cafeterias proudly promote the enticing dishes of traditional Dominican cuisine, which resembles Hispanic Caribbean and West Indian food in general but has undeniable differentiating characteristics.

On the average, a Dominican restaurant will sell *mangú*, a dish made out of boiled green plantain mashed with oil and sautéed onion. The tasty paste is accompanied by slices of avocado as well as fried eggs, salami, or "white cheese." Another common item, served with a variety of staples from white rice to boiled plantain, is deep-fried chopped chicken spiked with peppery seasonings. Dominicans call it *chicharrón de pollo*. Equally popular is *mondongo*, a lavishly seasoned heavy stew containing pig entrails. Served with white rice or root vegetables, it distantly resembles African American chitlins. *Chivo guisado*, made from goat meat stewed with spices, green peppers, and tomatoes, is often cooked on celebratory or festive occasions. Most meats invite the company of *tostones*, flattened slices of green plantain fried in oil and seasoned with salt, or of *moro*, rice made dark by mixing it with red or black beans and tomato sauce. Probably the most intricate dish in Dominican cuisine, and perhaps the best qualified to earn the title of national dish, is *sancocho*, a yellowish stew made with various kinds of meats, spices, yams, plantain, and other vegetables.

The following characterization offers a fair view of the cultural accent of Dominican food:

The flavor . . . starts with garlic, onions, coriander, and oregano. Similar to Cuban food, the basics include rice and beans. But Dominican cuisine has a distinct African flavor that distinguishes it from its more Spanish Cuban cousin. Its African origins are reflected in the use of more root vegetables and meats such as goat. (Bandon 1995: 100)

We may add that, in the United States, Dominican-owned cafeterias and restaurants combine the culinary resources of traditional American cuisine with the cooking styles, options, and preferences traceable to the Dominican Republic. Dominican food thus adds meaningfully to the diverse Hispanic kitchen on the United States. A close scrutiny of the eating habits of Dominicans in North America will most likely reveal that the community has widened the scope of its tastebuds to incorporate elements from other ethnic cuisines. The scrutiny will also most likely find that the diaspora has adopted styles and norms in the kitchen that were thought alien to Dominican cooking prior to migration. Delicious as Dominican food is, however, it remains relegated to the boundaries of the community. One will seldom find a Dominican restaurant in any mainstream neighborhood, including those in New York's Greenwich Village which owe their reputation to a sumptuous display of ethnic diversity. The hope is that as the Dominican community secures its enhanced visibility in the next decade, a greater number of people in the United States will get to enjoy the tasty creativity of Dominicans in the kitchen.

Of course, like everybody else, apart from food for the body, Dominicans also require nourishment for the soul. Back home, Dominicans are primarily Catholic with considerable numbers of people joining the many evangelical sects and Protestant churches that have extended their reach to the Dominican Republic. At the same time, the syncretic nature of Dominican cultures has allowed for the coexistence of Christianity with religious faiths of African origin. Thus, a large number of Dominicans who consider themselves Catholic practice vodou without any sense of contradiction (Deive 1992: 211). This popular religion—also spelled voodoo and vodun—is primarily associated with Haiti, but it can be found throughout the Caribbean and the United States in various forms. Deriving its name from the Dahomean word for "spirit," vodou draws on African and European beliefs. The *loa*, or spirit, plays a central role in vodou worship, which entails dance rituals and trances. Worshipers often become instruments (mediums) for the *loas* to manifest themselves through the process of epiphany or possession. In keeping with the syncretic nature of this folk religion, many *loas* descend directly from African deities, but some are indigenous to Haiti. Scholars have established the existence of a Dominican brand of vodou with characteristics of its own, including the incorporation of spiritual elements inherited from Taino culture.

Also, just as Haitian immigrants in the United States have brought along the religious practices of their native land, as Karen McCarthy Brown's *Mama Lola: A Vodou Priestess in Brooklyn* (1991) makes clear, at least one scholar has begun to document the presence of vodou among Dominicans in New York. Anthropologist Martha Ellen Davis, of the Center for Latin American Studies at the University of Florida, in Gainesville, contends that vodou is thriving among the members of the community largely as a traditional response to pressures stemming from the challenges of modern life and unfulfilled aspirations of first-generation immigrants. Davis argues that Dominican vodou worshipers in New York receive the spiritual influence of other African-descended religious expressions from the Caribbean, such as the Cuban *santería*, and that in the United States, as in the homeland, women retain the leadership in that folk religion. After migration to the United States, Dominicans retain their link with Catholic worship. Several local churches in New York, such as Incarnation, Saint Elizabeth, Saint Rose of Lima, and Saint Jude, have begun to function as "Dominican national parishes." Moreover, as educator Anneris Goris-Rosario has explained, Christian churches of other denominations, namely Pentecostal, Methodist, and Episcopal, have also become important for the spiritual and social life of the community. In Manhattan, Broadway Temple, a Methodist church, and St. Mary's Episcopal Church, have "gained respect in the community as religious institutions attentive to Dominican needs" (Goris-Rosario 1994: 34).

Dominican neighborhoods show the spiritual proclivity of the community rather visibly. A team of researchers conducting field research in Washington Heights found stickers with religious messages on many apartment doors in the area. Many Dominican homes and businesses display

small shrines with images of Catholic saints and the Virgin Mary in a corner of the hall or private room. These humble altars were usually surrounded by flowers, lighted candles, food, and glasses filled with fresh water, wines, and other alcoholic beverages. Although the most popular figures were the Virgin of Altagracia and Saint Lazarus, the altars represented a wide range of religious images: Saint Claire, Saint Anthony of Padua, Saint Barbara, the Holy Child of Atocha, the Sacred Heart, the Holy Family, and the Virgin of Fatima, among others. (Duany 1994: 23–24)

Similarly, some Dominicans in Washington Heights decorate their jewelry and adorn themselves with medals, scapulars, and rosaries carrying images of Christ or the Virgin.

Goris-Rosario has examined the identification of members of the clergy with the social needs and political causes affecting the Dominican community in New York. A case in point was a movement to protest the execution of Carlos Santana, a Dominican immigrant arrested in 1981 for participating in the robbery of an armored car in Houston, Texas. A security guard died in the assault, and conviction for the crime earned Santana capital punishment. During the week prior to Santana's execution, which would take place on Tuesday, March 29, 1993, Dominican activists, in collaboration with other Latinos, launched a series of public events aimed at influencing Texas authorities to order a stay of execution. Salient among the protests was a vigil that took place at Broadway Temple, which brought together many political leaders to participate in the religious services. Perhaps that political presence in the church suggests that for the Dominican community in New York the line separating "the sacred and the profane" may have started to "become blurred" (Goris-Rosario 1995: 138).

## GENDER

On the whole, as the foregoing discussion should suggest, Dominicans have invariably been active in asserting their presence socially and culturally in their immigrant abode. In that struggle for visibility, men and women have displayed equal dignity. Among the features that distinguish the Dominican experience in this country from the Dominican experience in the homeland is the heightened visibility of women as they share with men the leadership in the collective struggle for survival. The diaspora shows a keen awareness that men do not have a monopoly over the task of forging a destiny for the community. Indicative of the enhanced presence of women in public social functions is the spreading of institutions that focus specifically on women's concerns, such as the Dominican Women's Development Center, the Dominican Women's Caucus, and the Association of Progressive Women. Some organizations in Washington Heights provide guidance, counseling, and referrals to victims of domestic violence in the community, and many Dominican women know about the existence of those services as we gather from the testimony of a thirty-two-year-old single mother, Carmen Emilia Rodríguez, who now lives in Boston (Bandon 1995: 91). Worthy of note also are publications like *Mujer Latina*, a modest twelve-page magazine distributed in New York City that concentrates on disseminating information on the achievements of Hispanic women in the United States. The editor, Luz Sosa, is a Dominican, and so are many of the profiles of the women spotlighted in the magazine. The fall 1996 issue, for instance, highlighted the careers of Normandía Maldonado and Fabiola Feliz Soto. Maldonado is the founding director of a Dominican folk dance company called Ballet Quisqueya, which has represented the Dominican community at various Hispanic dance festivals since its founding in 1966. Soto, born in New York to Dominican parents who have lived in the city since 1940, is a civil court judge elected in the Bronx, "the first Dominican woman to be elected judge in the State," according to *Mujer Latina*.

Catering to a younger generation, the magazine *Mia*, edited by a young Dominican woman named Fabrienne Serignese, began in the summer of 1996 with a pilot issue and was released as a regular publication beginning in the fall of 1996. An English-language magazine, *Mia* caters to the youth culture of the hip-hop age with a focus on Latina women. That there should be Dominicans at the forefront of such initiatives speaks volumes for the activism of this community's women, young or old, in the United States. There is probably more than symbolic value in that *The Maria Paradox* (1996), a G. P. Putnam's Sons book that purports to teach U.S. Latina women how to overcome *marianismo*—a model of behavior that induces women to accept suffering and sacrifice passively and invariably defer to their men—was coauthored by Carmen Inoa Vásquez, a Dominican-born psychotherapist who teaches at the New York University School of Medicine and heads the clinical internship in psychology at Bellevue Hospital in New York City. On the whole, the reality of gender inequities and the need to forge models of relationships based on partnership rather than domination have become pressing issues for Dominicans in the United States.

## RACE

Race is another important area in which Dominicans find it necessary to adjust some of the social reflexes instilled by life on the native land. One may say that "Dominican society is the cradle of blackness in the Americas" since the island of Hispaniola "served as port of entry to the first African slaves who arrived in Spain's newly conquered territories following the transatlantic voyage of Christopher Columbus in 1492" (Torres-Saillant 1995: 110). A demographic assessment taking account of racial distinctions today would show that blacks and mulattoes make up nearly 90% of the Dominican Republic's close to eight million inhabitants. However, Dominicans have had to endure the aberrant negrophobia of the ruling class from colonial times to the present. Antiblack feeling has been promoted in the media, school textbooks, and speeches of some prominent political leaders. The dictatorship of Trujillo spent vast public resources in promoting an image of national identity that stressed the Hispanic European roots of the country's population and omitted any mention of an African heritage. Displayed in the library of the CUNY Dominican Studies Institute at City College is a white, blond, blue-eyed doll produced in the Dominican Republic for the export market in the 1940s as a representation of Dominican ethnicity. Joaquín Balaguer, a Trujillo associate who ruled the country during seven presidential terms from 1960 through 1996, even authored a book that in the 1980s overtly proclaimed the inferiority of blacks and urged Dominicans to strengthen their Spanish background (Balaguer 1984). The obnoxious racial lessons perpetrated by the Dominican ruling class have proven so enduring that still, in the summer of 1996, it seemed possible for conservative politicians and their liberal allies to use negrophobic discourse in the presidential campaign to defeat the popular black contender José Francisco Peña Gómez.

The members of the lower classes, the overwhelming majority of whom are of African descent, can do little to combat the media, the conservative intellectuals, and the school system. When Dominicans come to the United States, however, they escape the ideological artillery that sustains negrophobic thought in the homeland, and they have a greater possibility of coming to terms with their real ethnicity. In North America, a racially segregated society where the color of one's skin has often mattered more than the content of one's character in obtaining jobs and opportunities, Dominicans may find it expedient to assert their blackness. Cognizant that the larger white society

A Dominican face showing the community's characteristic racial hybridity. © Josefina Báez.

does not differentiate racially between them and Haitians or other dark-skinned Caribbeans, Dominicans become accustomed to speaking of themselves as a "people of color" and ally themselves with the other peoples of color in the struggle for survival. For instance, forty-two-year-old Rafael Guarnizo, a self-employed accountant who lives in Manhattan, refers to himself in a personal narrative as "being a black American, a Dominican American" (cited in Bandon 1995: 74). The assistant district attorney in Kings County, New York, is a young Dominican woman named Patria Frías who affirms her African heritage with conviction. Interviewed by *Raíces* (Watkins 1997: 19), a marginal magazine that seeks to bridge the gap between blacks and Latinos, Frías spoke about her refusal to remove her dreadlocks even though her hair style made some of her peers in the legal profession uncomfortable. Characteristically, one of her daughters is named Nairobi.

However, while some members of the community may go as far to uphold radically Afrocentric views of Dominican culture and ethnic identity, the common pattern is for them to recognize themselves as bearers of an alternative identity vis-à-vis the racial labels that predominate in the United States. "I was black to white America; I was some strange Spanish-speaking person to black America," says forty-year-old Rosa Bachleda, the Dominican founder in Chicago, Illinois, of an interracial group of women artists called Not Just Black and White (Bandon 1995: 59). But whatever specific language individual Dominicans may choose to articulate their racial or ethnic identity, they invariably overcome the legacy of denial regarding the African part of their heritage. That change most likely stems from their coming to environments where many of the darker peoples of the earth come together to share social space and fight for equality. Dominican children in New York generally attend the public school system, which is overwhelmingly populated by non-white students. In college too they go to institutions of higher education that are public. In New York specifically they have to interact on a daily basis with the majority of black, Latino, and Asian students who fill the classrooms of City University.

## DIASPORIC IDENTITY

In the United States, then, Dominicans begin to reconfigure their conception of cultural identity, reevaluating the issues of class, gender, and race. Many Dominicans in the diaspora commit themselves to challenging the assumptions contained in official definitions of Dominicanness as conveyed through the traditional textbooks. The CUNY Dominican Studies Institute has done much to disseminate information on Dominican history and culture in this country. In 1995 the Dominican Institute won a Rockefeller Foundation Humanities Fellowship award to finance a three-year residency program entitled "Representation versus Experience: Missing Chapters in Dominican History and Culture." The residency program allowed the institute to offer year-long appointments to scholars committed to

examine Dominican historiography and to stress those areas that have been least attended to by official Dominican historians, such as the role of women, the role of ordinary people in history, the role of the African heritage in Dominican society, the importance of rebellions and insurrections, the independence movements from within. (Luhrs 1997: 7)

It was arguably the experience of living as an ethnic minority in the United States that equipped the Dominican Institute leadership with the ideology of cultural authenticity implicit in the search for the "missing chapters." But, more important, chances are that a major Dominican research project that aims to dismantle negrophobic and elitist cultural discourse could have received approval only outside of the Dominican Republic, especially since the foundation awarded the grant while Balaguer still ruled as president of the country.

One of the most obvious results of the immigrant experience for Dominicans is that the space of their physical and existential mobility increases tremendously. Their living space after migration encompasses both the native country and the North American mainland. They now can access a larger mental habitat within which to configure their human identity. Their ampler sphere of experience entails an ability to harmonize English with Spanish, snowstorms with tropical rains, and merengue with rock or rap, to cite only a few divergent images. But it also entails the possibility of creating alternative models by rearranging the existing ones. Thus, there can be a Dominican young man who, though born in the United States, eats rice and beans and yearns to visit Santo Domingo in the summer, sitting right next to a middle-aged woman who has given up on Dominican food even though she came to this country only five years ago. The personal narratives contained in a recent book for young readers on Dominicans in the United States illustrate the diversity of profiles one can find in this community. Caonabo Pérez, a grocer in Washington Heights, came to this country in 1958. His U.S.-born and educated children mock him when he still speaks of returning to the Dominican Republic. Esperanza Herriarte operates a restaurant in Miami with her two sisters. She has a niece who attends Columbia University, in New York City, and plans to make her living as a writer in English. Agustín Trejo, a worker in a fish market in Providence, Rhode Island, came to this country illegally without knowing a word of English and after two years was engaged to marry a woman who had been born in this country (Bandon 1995: 16, 103, 50). These profiles reflect the fluid cultural contours that frame the life of the community.

Dominicans in the United States retain their simultaneous access to two geographies, nations, languages, and polities as parallel models in reference to which to articulate their concepts of self and society. Their cultural forms have become hybrid, shaped by what is retained from the homeland and what is acquired in the host country. Even something as basic as a bridal shower becomes a mixed cultural expression for Dominicans in New York; American and Dominican details fuse to become a third option (Bahn and Jaquez 1984: 140). According to Jorge Duany, "Transnational migration transforms social relations and generates a new identity that transcends traditional notions of physical and cultural space. Among other changes, the diaspora calls into question the immigrant's conception of ethnic, racial, and national identities as defined in their home countries" (Duany 1994: 46). Dominicans in the United States have developed cultural forms that without a doubt subvert the norms brought from the native land while simultaneously modifying the culture of the host country.

A Dominican girl wearing African-inspired braids, a sign of black affirmation.
© Josefina Báez.

# 5

# *The Future of Dominican Americans*

## NO LONGER BIRDS OF PASSAGE

Like most other ethnic segments of the U.S. population, Dominicans are busy at work in the effort to realize the dreams and aspirations that originally brought them to this country. They came to escape the throes of poverty and hopelessness. The earliest account of Dominican immigrants published in the New York press noted that in the Dominican Republic the poor had only three ways out of their social destitution: winning a lottery ticket, obtaining lucrative employment through political patronage, and leaving for the United States (Onis 1970: A3). But only a small number could realistically expect results from the first two options. The overwhelming majority chose to obtain visas to come to this country either as permanent residents or as tourists. In 1970 the Dominican presence in the United States elicited no perceptible concern. The Dominican government, whose economic policies turned emigration into a necessary survival strategy for the less empowered masses of the people, enjoyed the favor of the United States at the time. The *New York Times*, on May 19, 1970, on the occasion of his reelection as president of the Dominican Republic, nearly extolled Joaquín Balaguer in an article with the telling title of "Prudent Dominican Leader." The *Times* assessed him favorably even while acknowledging that the shrewd Trujillo associate accepted "frequent killings by the police" as "a fact of life" to ensure his own "political survival," kept "known killers on the payroll" to maintain opponents at bay, and employed public funds in construction contracts that meant to reward "political allies."

Expressions of concern over the growing size of the Dominican community in the receiving society began to manifest themselves in the mid-1970s, when it seems to have dawned on policy makers and immigration officials that the flow of Dominicans to the United States had developed a momentum of its own. In 1975 Maurice F. Kiley, district director of the Immigration and Naturalization Service, estimated at 1.5 million the number of illegal aliens in New York City, with Dominicans constituting as many as 200,000 of that total (A. Alvarez 1975: 25). Already authorities felt the need to check the increasingly thickening stream of migrants. Kiley explained the standard approach to applicants for tourist visas, many of whom overstayed their visit and later sought to become permanent: "Fifty per cent of all Dominicans who apply for non-immigrant visas are turned down. Those who do get in are peasants with borrowed suits. They rent 'show money' and obtain fraudulent documents to show they've been employed" (1975: 25).

Ironically, over two decades later, consular officials screening Dominican applicants still complained about their inability to curtail the passage of illegal visitors from the small Caribbean country. By February 1997, the U.S. consulate in the Dominican Republic was receiving over 500 requests for immigration and tourist visas daily. Clyde Howard, head of the nonimmigrant visa section, described the situation thus: "If we had the resources to investigate we'd probably find some element of fraud in the vast majority of cases. But you can't investigate everything" (Rohter 1997). While illegal migration has continued unabated for more than twenty years, the flow of legal immigration has continued to rise. According to a report issued in January 1997 by New York City's Department of City Planning, from 1990 to 1994 over 110,000 new immigrants from the Dominican Republic arrived in the city. In other words, one of every five new immigrants to the city was Dominican, showing a 50% increase over the rate of the previous decade.

The constant flow of Dominican immigrants—documented and undocumented—makes it difficult to determine the size of the community in the United States with any degree of accuracy. Nor does this scenario allow a stable profile to be drawn of the general characteristics of the community. Recent arrivals often share space with people who have lived in this country for twenty-five years or with U.S.-born Dominicans. A meeting at a cultural center or a community organization in a Dominican neighborhood may bring together a U.S.-educated college graduate who majored in English and a person who does not speak a word of English. The other instances of contrast at the meeting may include a conversation between a Dominican who still hopes to return to the home country to live permanently and another who identifies more closely with Latinos in the United States than with

Dominicans in the native land. That disparity pervades even the intimacy of the household. This situation was already perceptible in the mid-1970s, as we may gather from the testimony offered in 1975 by *New York Post* journalist Aida Alvarez of her interview with the de los Santos family in Queens, New York. The de los Santos family encouraged their U.S.-born daughters to speak Spanish, and the mother described a game she and her husband played with the girls: "Every once in a while we ask them—'What are you? Dominicans or Americans' Can you imagine, said the delighted mother, feigning astonishment, they answer, 'We're Americans' " (Alvarez 1975: 25).

Despite the varied self-perceptions and the disparities evident in the ways adult Dominicans might choose to define themselves nationally or culturally, the inexorable fact remains that the young see the United States as their unalienable home. Children born here or brought to this country prior to adolescence, educated and socialized in the United States, do not share the nostalgia of those older folks who might still hesitate to love this country as their own. Nearly ten years ago, in an appraisal of the conditions of Dominican immigrants, one of the coauthors of this book ventured a view of the future that bears quoting here, if anything to see how it compares with the vision that we might articulate today:

I personally hope in the near future to see more truly tangible signs that this community is perceiving New York as its home rather than a mere waiting room. I hope to see the day when these Dominicans will penetrate the construction industry and are able to help build their physical surroundings, the day when they will set up funeral homes and are able to die peacefully and bury their dead here. Signs of this kind will persuade me that Dominicans in the United States will have adapted to their new social milieu, having survived the alienation inherent in the immigrant experience, and engaged in a productive existence as a solid cultural group.

It is, I think, in the first generation of American born Dominicans that this hope should lie. They will have no excuse for doubting that this community is here to stay. For reasons which are peculiar to their own historical development, this generation will have no choice but to take in its own hands the reins of its destiny. Free from the tie to "la patria," these Dominican Americans will mentally be in the position to assert their presence as a New York minority and to wage a social battle for which their parents were inadequately equipped. Immigration is irreversible. Let us indulge in this cliché: you simply cannot go home again. Time, which is a great teacher, has amply demonstrated it. But, for Dominicans, the legacy of immigrants who came before, who paved the way, like Puerto Ricans, for example, has made the lesson a lot more clear. Hopefully, Dominican Americans, with a better sense of self-recognition, will be in closer contact with other Third World communities, enlarging thus their chance of discovering their true socio-cultural affinities. Should such a thing happen, Dominicans in the United States would be in a position to send to their relatives back in the island, not the fashionable shirt, the pair of sneakers, and the money order which have characterized the sending pattern of their parents, but instead a measure of that cultural identity which the bitter immigrant experience has forced them to acquire. (Torres-Saillant 1989: 23–24)

A decade after these words were written, we can account for important developments that amount to an improved positioning of Dominican attitudes regarding the appropriate ways to face the challenges posed by an ever more demanding, ever more competitive, American society. Dominicans cannot yet claim to have set a firm foot in the door of the construction industry or in any of the other heavy economic areas that require influence and clout. But they seem meaningfully invested in the effort to acquire a measure of political power. Though modest, their achievements in education deserve mention. Their business entrepreneurs have displayed their fair share of capitalist instinct as they vie for a space in the U.S. economy. Similarly, they have gradually increased their visibility in the arts, popular music, literature, and other cultural expressions.

At the grassroots level, community efforts have brought about the naming of several northern Manhattan public schools after important Dominican figures: Juan Pablo Duarte, Gregorio Luperón, Salomé Ureña, and Hermanas Mirabal. Getting non-Dominican school authorities in the school districts and at the central administration of the Board of Education to approve the alien names of historical characters from the Dominican Republic invariably entailed a mastery of organizational skills. The coordinators of each individual campaign to promote the names had to convene large numbers of area residents to rally around their cause, showing the political aptitude required for successful lobbying before public institutions. The significance of those symbolic gains matters all the more in light of the negligible presence of Dominicans in policy-making positions in the community school districts that serve their children. One could speculate that within another decade the gains will have gone beyond the realm of the symbolic, and the scenario will show such concrete advancements as a greater proportion of Dominican licensed teachers, several school superintendents of Dominican descent, and an enhanced representation of Dominican history and culture in the curriculum.

## THE ANTI-IMMIGRANT WAVE

Dominicans in the United States face all the obstacles historically encountered by nonwhite ethnic minorities. Coming from a Spanish-speaking region of the Third World, Dominicans share the plight of U.S. Hispanics whom many viewed as the principal target of the animosity toward immigrants prevailing in the land during the 1990s. With the advent of a new wave of conservative politicians who became a majority in the Congress in 1992, a discourse of antipathy against nonwhite foreigners gained currency. However, the sentiment conveyed in the phrase "not this time José," whereby Patrick Buchanan summarized his proposed immigration policy during his bid for the Republican presidential nomination in the 1996 election, evinced a disposition to single out Hispanics. At the same time, the English-only movement, which many Latinos see as a cultural offensive directed specifically at them, received added strength in various cities and states throughout the nation. In Amarillo, Texas, to cite just one extreme example, state district court judge Samuel C. Kiser construed a mother's decision to speak Spanish to her daughter as a case of child abuse. As reported in New York by the short-lived bilingual newspaper *El Daily News* on August 30, 1995, judge Kiser ruled against Martha Laureano in a custody case and favored the father's claim that speaking to the daughter in Spanish was tantamount to disabling her socially.

Nor it is just the language that has earned Latinos contempt from conservative quarters. Francis (Bud) Wassner, mayor of the suburban village of Haverstraw, New York, went as far as to suggest that mostly everything about them is a problem. Hispanic immigrants, mostly Dominicans, Cubans, and Puerto Ricans, made up 51% of the village's population according to the 1990 Census. Mayor Wassner regretted that "Haverstraw is better known in the islands than in New York City" (Ojito 1996: B2). He contended that Hispanic immigrants crowded the streets, putting a serious burden on local resources since the police had to spend an enormous amount of time and effort "to keep them off the streets as much as it is legally possible." Furthermore, the mayor objected to the Hispanic presence in his village because of the sanitation problems he felt they caused: "They produce a lot of garbage. I mean, rice and beans are heavy, you know" (1996: B2).

One could argue that Judge Kiser and Mayor Wassner's pronouncements were encouraged by an overall climate that fostered ethnocentric sentiments. They came in the wake of the rise of prominent conservative voices in Washington, D.C., whose moral leadership gradually found echo even among many legislators who had formerly held liberal views. In that context, a few social ideals that had long been seen as integral to the American democracy began to be revisited. The constitutionally sanctioned principle of *jus solis*, which established that being born in U.S. territory automatically made the person an American citizen, was called into question by a strong faction of

A mostly Dominican audience at gala screening in New York City of *Un pasaje de ida* (A One-Way Ticket), a movie about the tragedy of illegal emigration from the Dominican Republic. © Eduardo Hoepelman, courtesy of Dominican Studies Institute archives.

the legislature. They began to promote the idea of an amendment to the U.S. Constitution with an eye on denying the right of citizenship to the U.S.-born children of undocumented aliens.

Consistent with the overall ambiance that made immigrant bashing fashionable in 1996, the Immigration and Naturalization Service put into effect several aspects of a new immigration law that has serious consequences for undocumented as well as for legal aliens. The combination of the immigration regulation with an Anti-terrorist Act increased the grounds for deporting foreigners. Many Dominicans, even those with over fifteen years of permanent residence in the United States, found themselves barred from reentry on their way back from family-related or vacation trips to the Dominican Republic. Despite the longevity of their status as legal residents of the United States, return travelers were subjected to the same close scrutiny normally applied to someone coming into the country for the first time. If, upon an elaborate computer search of the returnee's records, the immigration officer found any violation of the law, including in some cases unpaid parking tickets or alimony payment arrears, the officer would have the culprit immediately sent to a detention center to begin the process of deportation.

Worsening the effects of the new immigration ruling, a new welfare law was approved in 1996 with unfavorable consequences for noncitizens. The revamping of welfare, among other things, made it difficult for legal U.S. residents to qualify for social services. Despite their long stay as law-abiding tax-paying legal aliens, noncitizens ceased to qualify for disability benefits and food stamps. Such was the case of Juan Tomás Abreu, a Dominican immigrant included among four plaintiffs represented by the nonprofit New York Legal Assistance Group, an advocacy organization that sought to challenge the legality of the new welfare rules. A former tax-paying garment worker, Abreu suffered a brain hemorrhage before he could meet the five-year residency requirement to file for naturalization. As a result, in 1997, lying in coma for more than five years, Abreu faced the loss of the $570 per month disability compensation he got from the federal government. If the claim of the new welfare rules' unconstitutionality did not succeed, Abreu would be among 86,000 elderly and disabled legal immigrants in New York City scheduled to lose their benefits as of August 1997 (Gordy 1997: 4).

As the case of Abreu dramatically illustrates, it is unsafe for a Dominican in the United States to live without the protection of a citizenship status. That the members of the community understand their predicament may be deduced from the large numbers of Dominican immigrants who over the last several years have sought to become naturalized. However, not all who wish to become citizens may do so successfully. Many reasons exist to deny a person his or her citizenship application. In many cases, filing for naturalization can result in the outright deportation of an individual. As the Washington-based Dominican analyst Roberto Alvarez has observed, the new immigration law includes a provision that allows for the retroactive deportation of legal aliens who have a criminal record. The measure applies even if the immigrant committed the crime five or ten years back, paid for it by serving time in prison or fulfilling any other appropriate penalty, and has since then led an exemplary life as a law-abiding, legal resident of the United States (R. Alvarez 1997: 37).

## THE TENSION OF HERE AND THERE

Even as they wrestle with the imperative of citizenship and the concomitant conflicts, Dominicans must endeavor to negotiate the tension inherent in their dual access to the politics of both U.S. and Dominican societies. Many would contend that the future well-being of the community will depend largely on its ability to articulate a kind of interaction with the home country that will not hamper its insertion into the more urgent political reality of the host country. Consistent with the advent of the global economy, many Dominicans have settled into a mode that scholars have described as a transnational identity, a cultural state of mind that permits them to remain actively linked to life in the native land while also becoming acclimated to the values and norms of the receiving society. However, one wonders whether a community can efficaciously sustain the level of concentration necessary for defending its interests as well as uphold its economic and political rights simultaneously in two societies. One could fear that the need to remain focused on multiple goings-on in divergent political systems of separate geographies may cause Dominicans to spread themselves thin.

The concern over the political duality of U.S. Dominicans has become particularly tangible in light of a 1996 amendment to the Constitution of the Dominican Republic, which decreed the retention of citizenship rights and privileges for all people born in the Dominican Republic who had become citizens of another country. The measure will most likely benefit the small country's economy insofar as Dominican-born U.S. citizens, freed from the higher rate of taxation applied to foreigners, may be lured to buy property or otherwise invest in a society whose economy is partly dependent on the remittances of Dominicans living in the United States. The added incentive, plus the growing currency of a movement that aims to enable Dominicans abroad to participate directly in the republic's electoral proceedings by casting their ballots at polls placed in Dominican consular offices in cities throughout the world, is likely to tie the U.S. Dominican community ever more firmly to the day-to-day political affairs of their native land. Time will tell whether the status of dual citizenship can be deemed as a strength or as a sort of political distraction lessening the Dominican community's concentration on immediate matters that effect them in the American society. Should the participation of U.S. Dominicans in electoral processes of the island become a reality, one can expect a further complication of the political situation of the community. As Assemblyman Adriano Espaillat has intimated, U.S. Dominicans might import the party rivalries, adversarial factions, and group interests that are associated with politics in the Dominican Republic, adding potentially divisive variables that may contribute to fragmentation in the community. Another concern is that party leaders from the homeland may step up their fund-raising efforts among the immigrants. Already some community observers hold the view that island politicians treat the Dominican diaspora in the United States as an inexhaustible coffer from which they draw all too often, resulting in a divestment of resources away from neighborhoods that need them badly.

## THE OBSTACLE OF RACE

In addition to the obstacles stemming from the language barrier and an often unfavorable immigration status, Dominicans face an impediment that they share with most other communities of color in the United States, namely racism. Generally darker than Cubans, Puerto Ricans, and most other Latinos, Dominicans bear the brunt of a history of negrophobia whose vestiges still persist in American society. Ironically, it is neither the unskilled nor blue-collar workers who most dramatically suffer the oppressive weight of racial discrimination. Their own social segregation, their confinement to labor markets populated mostly by their own people, keeps them for the most part from stepping outside their immediate ethnic milieu. As they hardly ever get to interact with people from the dominant sectors of society, they stay largely away from the settings where the drama of racism can be felt directly. It is really the professionals and those most qualified to compete for employment, education, and commercial opportunities in the mainstream who feel it in their flesh. It is they who get the chance to experience personally the extent to which their phenotype can limit their aspirations.

The case of young Dominican professional Heriberto Cabrera provides a pertinent example of this phenomenon. Cabrera received part of his education in a seminary before attending Boston College. After law school, he chose to work in the office of the Manhattan district attorney. However, he is hardly doing well in his chosen profession. Money continues to pose problems, and the big, lucrative cases elude him. He and his wife have two children, and the worry of insecurity sets in, to the point that he often wakes up in the middle of the night covered with sweat: "He remembers himself holding on, knowing that if he let go, he'd die. It is a recurring dream" (Shorris 1992: 328). The inability of Dominican and other young Latino lawyers to become partners in large law firms points to a dismal scenario for someone like Cabrera. "The notion that bright, well-educated Latinos can write their own ticket in the business world is a myth, especially in the legal profession, where the rules of racism are applied with the kind of precision characteristic of the best legal minds" (1992: 329).

## HOPING FOR THE BEST

In closing, after three decades of massive and continuous migration to the United States, Dominicans have, even if precariously, taken decisive steps toward their insertion into the fabric of American life. Seen against the backdrop of a shrinking economy and a political ambiance that has turned inhospitable for the immigrant, Dominicans face added challenges to their survival as a vibrant ethnic community in the United States. However, the history of the Dominican people both in their country of origin and in the United States shows that they have the capacity to live through the best of times and the worst of times. Such fitness for survival was demonstrated by the Almonte family, whose journey from the backland village of Camu in northern Dominican Republic to the wondrous metropolis of New York City became the subject of the twelve-part monthly series "A Chronicle of Hope: The Odyssey of the Almonte Family," published by the daily *New York Newsday* beginning on April 27, 1986.

Since then, the author of the series, Barbara Fischkin, has turned her articles into a book, *Muddy Cup* (1997). The Almontes are an ordinary Dominican immigrant family from a rural background, and the trials they underwent realistically represent the challenges that the community confronts on a daily basis. Given the precarious lives they led in Camu and the relative gains they have achieved since the early 1980s, when the members of the family began to head for New York, one must say they have improved their lot. Though they have suffered major losses as a result of their painful uprooting from their homeland and the difficulty of adjusting to the United States, they own their own home in Queens, they have acquired some assets in their hometown, and at least one of their four children has done well enough academically to pursue graduate studies. A work ethic informed the father, and a bit of luck helped him get a job as a carpenter when he first arrived in New York. The mother, on the other hand, had a pliable soul, which equipped her with a tremendous ability to bend, sacrifice, and adjust to change. That combination of qualities proved decisive in ensuring the family's survival. For those unassisted by a comparable combination of qualities, one may simply, even if defying logic, hope for the best.

# Bibliography

Abreu, Alfonso, et al. *Las zonas francas industriales: El éxito de una politica económica.* Santo Domingo: Editora Corripio, 1989.

Alvarez, Aida. "New York's Latins: The Dominicans." *New York Post,* February 24, 1975: 25.

Alvarez, Roberto. "Emigración legal e ilegal de dominicanos hacia E.U." *Rumbo* 4, no. 171 (1997): 34–39.

Anon. *Santo Domingo: A Brief Sketch of the Island, Its Resources, and Commercial Possibilities with Special Reference to the Treaty Now Pending in the United States Senate.* New York: New York Commercial, 1906.

Aponte, Sarah. *Dominican Migration to the United States, 1970–1997: An Annotated Bibliography.* New York: CUNY Dominican Studies Institute, forthcoming.

Ariza Castillo, Marina, et al. *Población, migraciones internas y desarrollo en la República Dominicana 1950–1981.* Santo Domingo: Impresos Profesionales, C. por A., 1991.

Augenbraum, Harold, and Margarite Fernández Olmos, eds. *The Latino Reader: An American Literary Tradition.* Boston: Houghton Mifflin Co., 1997.

Austerlitz, Paul. *Merengue: Dominican Music and Dominican Identity.* Philadelphia: Temple University Press, 1997.

Báez Everstz, Franc, and Frank Ramírez D'Oleo. *La emigración de dominicanos a los Estados Unidos.* Santo Domingo: Fundación Friedrich Ebert, 1985.

Bahn, Adele, and Angela Jaquez. "One Style of Dominican Bridal Shower." In *The Apple Sliced: Sociological Studies of New York City,* edited by Vernon Boggs, Gerald Handel, and Sylvia F. Fava, 131–46. New York: Praeger, 1984.

Balaguer, Joaquín. *La isla al revés: Haiti y el destino dominicano.* 2d ed. Santo Domingo: Librería Dominicana, 1984.

Balcácer, Juan D., and Manuel A. García. *La independencia dominicana*. Madrid: Editorial Mapfre, 1992.

Bandon, Alexandra. *Dominican Americans*. Footsteps to America series. Parsippany, N.J.: New Discovery Books, 1995.

Bobadilla, Tomás, et al. "Manifiesto de los pueblos de la parte Este de la isla antes Española o de Santo Domingo, sobre las causas de su separación de la República Haitiana." In *La independencia dominicana*, edited by Juan D. Balcácer and Manuel A. García, 219–26. Madrid: Editorial Mapfre, 1992.

Bray, David. "Economic Development: The Middle Class and International Migration in the Dominican Republic." *International Migration Review* 18, no. 2 (1984): 217–36.

———. "The Dominican Exodus: Origins, Problems, and Solutions." In *The Caribbean Exodus*, edited by Barry B. Levine, 152–70. New York: Praeger, 1987.

Brown, Karen McCarthy. *Mama Lola: A Vodou Priestess in Brooklyn*. Berkeley: University of California Press, 1991.

Brown, Wenzell. *Angry Men, Laughing Men: The Caribbean Cauldron*. New York: Greenberg Publisher, 1947.

Burma, John H. *Spanish-Speaking People in the United States*. Durham, N.C.: Duke University Press, 1954.

Calder, Bruce. *The Impact of Intervention: The Dominican Republic during the U.S. Occupation of 1916–1924*. Austin: University of Texas Press, 1984.

Calvo, Félix, and Haroldo Dilla. *Crisis del desarrollismo, auge del monetarismo*. Santo Domingo: Editora Taller, 1986.

Camacho, Jhovanny. "Dominican Memorial Art: Testimonials of Pain in a Diaspora." *Punto 7 Review: A Journal of Marginal Discourse* 3, no. 1 (1996): 126–34.

Candelario, Ginetta E. B., and Nancy López. "The Latest Edition of the Welfare Queen Story." *Phoebe: Journal of Feminist Scholarship, Theory, and Aesthetics* 7, nos. 1–2 (1995): 7–22.

Caram de Alvarez, Magaly. "Cambios en los patrones reproductivos de la familia dominicana." *Población y Sociedad* 1(1991): 43–60.

Carrasquillo, Angela L., and Clement B. London. *Parents and Schools: A Source Book*. New York: Garland Publishing, 1993.

Casares, Eduardo. "Preface." *Art in Transit: A Dominican Experience*. New York: INTAR Latin American Gallery, 1996.

Cassá, Roberto. *Capitalismo y dictadura*. Santo Domingo: Universidad Autónoma de Santo Domingo, 1982.

Ceara Hatton, Miguel. *Tendencias estructurales y coyuntura de la economía dominicana 1968–1983*. Santo Domingo: Centro de Investigación Económica (CIECA), 1990a.

———. *Crecimiento económico y acumulación de capital: Consideraciones teóricas y empíricas en la República Dominicana*. Santo Domingo: Universidad Iberoamericana UNIBE, 1990b.

Ceara Hatton, Miguel, and Edwin Croes Hernández. *El gasto público social de la República Dominicana en la década de los ochentas.* Santo Domingo: Centro de Investigaciones Económica y Fondo de las Naciones Unidas para la Infancia (UNICEF), 1993.

Ceara Hatton, Miguel, et al. *Hacia una reestructuración dirigida de la economía dominicana.* Santo Domingo: Fundación Friedrich Ebert, 1986.

Cela, Jorge, Isis Duarte, and Carmen J. Gómez. *Población, crecimiento urbano y barrios marginados en Santo Domingo.* Santo Domingo: Fundación Friedrich Ebert, 1988.

Chávez, Linda. *Out of the Barrio: Toward a New Politics of Hispanic Assimilation.* New York: Basic Books, 1991.

City University of New York. *Immigration/Migration and the CUNY Student of the Future.* New York: CUNY, 1995.

Columbus, Christopher. *Journal of the First Voyage* (Diario del primer viaje). Edited and translated by B. W. Ife. Warminster: Aris and Phillis, 1990.

Courtney, W. S. *The Gold Fields of Santo Domingo.* New York: Anson P. Norton, 1860.

Cruz Almánzar, Amín. *Periodismo dominicano en New York: Fundamentos, evolución, vicisitudes y futuro.* New York: Editorial Arce, 1993.

De Rege, Carlo. "Dominicans Are Coming to New York." *Migration Today* 2, no. 4 (1974): 1, 8.

Deive, Carlos Esteban. *Vodú y magia en Santo Domingo.* 3d. ed. Santo Domingo: Fundación Cultural Dominicana, 1992.

Del Castillo, José, and Manuel A. García Arévalo. *Antología del merengue.* Santo Domingo: Banco Antillano, S.A., 1988.

Del Castillo, José, and Christopher Mitchell. *La inmigración dominicana en los Estados Unidos.* Santo Domingo: CENAPEC, 1987.

Del Castillo, José, et al. *La Gulf y Western en República Dominicana.* Santo Domingo: Editora de la UASD, 1974.

Del Rosario Mota, Gumersindo, and Patria Stella Madera Daniel. "Cambios en los niveles de y patrones de consumo, según estratos poblacionales de ingreso, 1976–1977." In *Forum* no. 12. *Población y Pobreza en la República Dominicana,* edited by Frank Moya Pons, 97–156. Santo Domingo: Forum, 1984.

Department of City Planning. *Annual Report on Social Indicators.* New York City, 1991.

———. *The Newest New Yorkers: An Analysis of Immigration into New York City during the 1980s.* New York City, 1992.

———. *The Newest New Yorkers: A Statistical Portrait.* New York City, 1992.

———. New Opportunities for a Changing Economy: Summary Report of the Citywide Industry Study. New York City, 1993.

Díaz, Mariano. "The Independent Supermarket and Inner City Retailing." Sixth

Annual NSA Banquet. *The National Supermarkets Association.* November 11, 1995.

D'Oleo, Frank. "1990: Crisis agraria, dominación agroindustrial y descampesinización." *Análisis de Coyuntura* 3, no. 6 (1991): 1–62.

Drennan, Matthew. "The Decline and Rise of the New York Economy." In *Dual City: Restructuring New York.* Edited by John H. Mollenkopf and Manuel Castells. New York: Russell Sage Foundation, 1991.

Duany, Jorge. "De la periferia a la semi-periferia: La migración dominicana hacia Puerto Rico." In *Los Dominicanos en Puerto Rico: Migración en la semi-periferia.* Edited by Jorge Duany, 26–46. San Juan, Puerto Rico: Ediciones Huracán, 1990.

———. *Quisqueya on the Hudson: The Transnational Identity of Dominicans in Washington Heights.* Dominican Research Monographs. New York: CUNY Dominican Studies Institute, 1994.

Duarte, Isis. *Trabajadores urbanos: Ensayos sobre fuerza laboral en República Dominicana.* Santo Domingo: Editora Universitaria (UASD), 1986.

Duarte, Isis, and André Corten. "Proceso de proletarización de mujeres. Las trabajadoras de industria de ensamblaje en República Dominicana." Universidad Antónoma de Santo Domingo. Typescript. 1982.

Duarte, Rosa. *Apuntes de Rosa Duarte.* Edited by E. Rodríguez Demorizi, C. Larrazábal Blanco, and V. Alfau Durán. 2d ed. Santo Domingo: Secretaría de Estado de Educación Bellas Artes y Cultos, 1994.

Duffy, Martha. "Mais Oui, Oscar!" *Time,* February 8, 1993, 68–70.

The Economist. *Book of Vital World Statistics: A Portrait of Everything Significant in the World Today.* New York: Times Books, a division of Random House, 1990.

Fabens, Joseph Warren. *In the Tropics. By a Settler in Santo Domingo.* Introduction by Richard B. Kimball. New York: Carleton, 1863.

———. *Life in Santo Domingo. By a Settler.* Introduction by Richard B. Kimball. New York: Carleton, 1873.

Falcón, Angelo, and Christopher Hanson Sánchez. *Latino Immigrants and Electoral Participation.* New York: Institute for Puerto Rican Policy, 1996.

Fernández, Roberta, ed. *In Other Words: Literature by Latinas of the United States.* Houston: Arte Público Press, 1994.

Fischkin, Barbara. *Muddy Cup: A Dominican Family Comes of Age in a New America.* New York: Scribner, 1997.

Frank Canelo, J. *Dónde, porqué, de qué y cómo viven los dominicanos en el extranjero: Un informe sociológico sobre la inmigración dominicana, 1961–82.* Santo Domingo: Alfa y Omega, 1982.

Galeano, Eduardo. *Open Veins of Latin America: Five Centuries of the Pillage of a Continent.* New York: Monthly Review Press, 1973.

"The Galíndez Mystery and the Trujillo Horror." *National Guardian,* June 1956, 3.

Galíndez, Jesús de. *The Era of Trujillo, Dominican Dictator*. Tucson: University of Arizona Press, 1973.

Garrison, Vivian, and Claudewell S. Thomas. "A Case of a Dominican Migrant." In *Alienation in Contemporary Society: A Multidisciplinary Examination*. Edited by Roy S. Brycc-Laporte and Claudewell S. Thomas, 216–60. New York: Praeger, 1976.

Garrison, Vivian, and Carol I. Weiss. "Dominican Family Networks and United States Immigration Policy: A Case Study." In *Caribbean Life in New York City: Sociocultural Dimensions*. Edited by Constance R. Sutton and Elsa M. Chaney, 235–54. New York: Center for Migration Studies, 1987.

Georges, Eugenia. *The Making of a Transnational Community: Migration, Development, and Cultural Change in the Dominican Republic*. New York: Columbia University Press, 1990.

———. *Ethnic Associations and the Integration of New Immigrants: Dominicans in New York City*. Occasional Paper no. 41. New York Research Program in Inter-American Affairs, 1984.

Gómez, Carmen J., and Clara Báez. "Mujer y trabajo." *Población y Desarrollo* 23 (1988): 1–38.

González, David. "Unmasking Roots of Washington Heights Violence." *New York Times*, October 17, 1993, Metro Section, B1, 29, 34.

González, Nancie. "Peasants' Progress: Dominicans in New York." *Caribbean Studies* 10, no. 3 (1970): 154–71.

———. "Multiple Migratory Experiences of Dominicans in New York." *Anthropological Quarterly* 49, no. 1 (1976): 36–43.

Gordon, Andrew J. "Hispanic Drinking after Migration: The Case of Dominicans." *Medical Anthropology* 2, no. 4 (1978): 61–84.

Gordy, Molly. "U.S. Pens 'Citizen Pain'." *New York Daily News*, March 26, 1997, 4.

Goris-Rosario, Anneris. "The Role of the Ethnic Community and the Workplace in the Integration of Immigrants: A Case Study of Dominicans in New York City." Ph.D. Diss., Fordham University, New York, 1994.

———. "Rites for a Rising Nationalism: Religious Meaning and Dominican Community Identity in New York City." In *Old Masks, New Faces: Religion and Latino Identities*, edited by Anthony M. Stevens-Arroyo and Gilbert R. Cadena, 117–41. PARAL Studies Series. Vol.2. New York: Bildner Center for Western Hemisphere Studies, 1995.

Grasmuck, Sherri. "The Consequences of Dominican Urban Out-migration for National Development: The Case of Santiago." In *The Americas in the New International Division of Labor*, edited by S. Sanderson, 145–76. New York: Holmes & Meier, 1985.

Grasmuck, Sherri, and Patricia R. Pessar. *Between Two Islands: Dominican International Migration*. Berkeley: University of California Press, 1991.

Guarnizo, Luis. "One Country in Two: Dominican-owned Firms in New York and in the Dominican Republic." Ph.D. Diss., Johns Hopkins University, Baltimore, 1993.

Gurak, D., and Mary Kritz. "Dominican and Colombian Women in New York City: Household Structure and Employment Patterns." *Migration Today* 10 (1982): 14–21.

Hancock, Henry J. "The Situation in Santo Domingo." *Annals of the American Academy of Political and Social Science* 463 (1905): 47–52.

Hanley, Elizabeth. "Milly's Merengue." *Mother Jones* 16 (1991): 44–45.

Hazard, Samuel. *Santo Domingo, Past and Present, with a Glance at Haiti.* New York: Harper and Brothers, 1873.

Hendricks, Glenn T. *The Dominican Diaspora: From the Dominican Republic to New York City. Villagers in Transition.* New York: Teachers College Press, 1974.

Henríquez Ureña, Max, ed. *Pedro Henríquez Ureña: Antología.* Colección Pensamiento Dominicano. Ciudad Trujillo: Librería Dominicana, 1950.

Henríquez y Carvajal, Francisco. "De Francisco Henríquez y Carvajal a Pedro Henríquez Ureña." *Familia Henríquez Ureña: Epistolario,* 657–58. Publicaciones del Sesquicentenario de la Independencia Nacional. Santo Domingo: Secretaría de Estado de Educación, Bellas Artes y Cultos, 1994.

Hernández, Ramona, and Nancy López. "Yola and Gender: Dominican Women's Unregulated Migration." In *Dominican Studies: Resources and Research Questions,* Luis Alvarez-López, et al., 59–78. New York: CUNY Dominican Studies Institute at City College, 1997.

Hernández, Ramona, Francisco Rivera-Batiz, and Roberto Agodini. *Dominican New Yorkers: A Socioeconomic Profile, 1990.* New York: CUNY Dominican Studies Institute, 1995.

Hernández, Ramona, and Silvio Torres-Saillant. "Dominicans in New York: Men, Women, and Prospects." In *Latinos in New York: Communities in Transition.* Edited by Gabriel Haslip Viera and Sherrie Baver, 30–56. Notre Dame: University of Notre Dame Press, 1996.

Hicks, Albert C. *Blood in the Streets: The Life and Rule of Trujillo.* Introduction by Quentin Reynolds. New York: Creative Age Press, 1946.

History and Migration Task Force, Centro de Estudios Puertorriqueños. *Labor Migration Under Capitalism: The Puerto Rican Experience.* New York: Monthly Review Press, 1979.

Hoetink, Harry. "Los americanos de Samaná." *Eme Eme: Estudios Dominicanos* 2, no. 10 (1974): 3–26.

Holm, John. *Pidgins and Creoles.* Vol. 2. Cambridge, England: Cambridge University Press, 1989.

Holston, Mark. "The Women of Merengue." *Américas* 42, no. 3 (1990): 54–55.

Immigration and Naturalization Service (INS). 1960–1991 Annual Reports. Washington, D.C.: U.S. Government Printing Office.

Inchaústegui, Arístides. *Por amor al arte: Notas sobre música, compositores e intérpretes dominicanos.* Santo Domingo: Secretaría de Estado de Educación Bellas Artes y Cultos, 1995.

Jordan, Howard. "Dominicans in New York: Getting a Slice of the Apple." *NACLA Report on the Americas* 30, no. 5 (1997): 37–42.

Junco, Maité. "For Dominican Immigrants the American Dream Lives On." *New York Daily News,* January 9, 1997, 1, 4–5.

Kanellos, Nicolás. *The Hispanic Almanac: From Columbus to Corporate America.* Detroit: Visible Ink Press, 1994.

———, ed. *The Hispanic Literary Companion.* Detroit: Visible Ink Press, 1997.

Kaplan, Stephen D. "The Shaping of Contemporary Dominican Art." In *Art in Transit: A Dominican Experience,* 13–16. New York: INTAR Latin American Gallery, 1996.

Kasarda, D. John. "Caught in the Web of Change." *Society* 21 (1983): 4–7.

———. "Structural Factors Affecting the Location and Timing of Urban Underclass Growth." *Urban Geography* 11, no. 3 (1990): 237–53.

Keim, Deb Randolph. *Santo Domingo.* Philadelphia: Claxton, Remsen, and Haffelfinger, 1870.

King, Lourdes Miranda. "The Spanish-Speaking American." In *Ethnic American Minorities: A Guide to Media and Materials,* edited by Harry A. Johnson, 189–239. New York: R. R. Bowker, 1976.

Knight, Melvin M. *The Americans in Santo Domingo.* Studies in American Imperialism. New York: Vanguard Press, 1928.

Levy, Clifford J. "A Racial Study Finds Differences in Jail Sentences." *New York Times,* April 10, 1996, B1.

Lobo, Arun Peter, and Joseph J. Salvo. "Immigration to New York City in the 1990s: The Saga Continues." *Migration World Magazine* 25, no. 3 (1997): 14–17.

Loucky, James. Review of *Sugarball: The American Game, The Dominican Dream,* by Alan M. Klein. *American Anthropologist* 94, no. 2 (1992): 956–57.

Lozano, Wilfredo. *El reformismo dependiente.* Santo Domingo: Editora Taller, 1985.

Luhrs, Joyce. "A Dominican Place in the Sun: Research Institute Illuminates Past and Present." *Hispanic Outlook on Higher Education* 7, no. 15 (1997): 7–8.

McAlary, Mike. "Washington Heights' Deadly Dominican Connection." *New York Post,* September 6, 1992: 3.

———. "The Framing of a Cop." *New York Post,* October 9, 1991: 2, 21.

McDonald, Brian. "The Rise and Fall of El Feo." *New York Times,* September 15, 1996, Section 13, The City, 1, 12–13.

Manzueta Martínez, E. "Francamente dominicana." *Revista Económica del Listín Diario,* January 1994: 2.

Marini, Ruy Mauro. "Dialéctica de la dependencia: La economía exportadora." In *Tres ensayos sobre América Latina.* Edited by Rodolfo Stavenhagen, Ernesto Laclau, and Ruy Mauro Marini, 91–135. Barcelona: Editora Anagrama, 1973.

Martin, John Bartlow. *Overtaken by Events: The Dominican Crisis from the Fall of Trujillo to the Civil War.* New York: Doubleday, 1966.

Meillassoux, Claude. *Maidens, Meal, and Money: Capitalism and the Domestic Community.* Cambridge, England: Cambridge University Press, 1981.

Miller, Jeanette. *Historia de la pintura dominicana.* 3d. ed. Santo Domingo: n.p., 1984.

Miller, Wayne Charles. *A Comprehensive Bibliography for the Study of American Minorities.* Vol. 2. New York: New York University Press, 1976.

Mills, C. Wright. *White Collar: The American Middle Classes.* New York: Oxford University Press, 1951.

Mills, C. Wright, Clarence Senior, and Rose Goldsen. *The Puerto Rican Journey: New York's Newest Migrants.* New York: Harper & Bros, 1950.

Miolán, Angel. *El perredé desde mi ángulo: Páginas históricas.* 2d ed. Caracas: Avila Arte, S.A., 1985.

Mitchell, Christopher. "U.S. Foreign Policy and Dominican Migration to the United States." *Western Hemisphere Immigration and United States Foreign Policy,* edited by Christopher Mitchell, 89–124. University Park: Pennsylvania State University Press, 1992.

Moya Pons, Frank. *La dominación haitiana: 1822–1844.* Santiago: Universidad Católica Madre y Maestra, 1972.

———. *Manual de historia dominicana.* Santiago: Universidad Católica Madre y Maestra, 1977.

———. *Empresarios en conflicto: política de industrialización y sustitución de importaciones en la República Dominicana.* Santo Domingo: Fondo para el Avance de las Ciencias Sociales, 1992.

———. "La migración exagerada." *Rumbo* 1, no. 10 (1994): 6.

———. *The Dominican Republic: A National History.* New Rochelle, N.Y.: Hispaniola Books, 1995.

Munro, Dana G. *Intervention and Dollar Diplomacy in the Caribbean: 1900–1921.* Princeton, N.J.: Princeton University Press, 1964.

Navarro, Mireya. "An Actress Openly Faces AIDS and Receives an Audience's Ovation." *New York Times,* December 5, 1993, Sunday ed.

Nelson, William Javier. *Almost a Territory: America's Attempt to Annex the Dominican Republic.* Newark: University of Delaware Press, 1990.

Novas, Himilce. *The Hispanic 100.* New York: Carol Publishing, 1995.

Núñez de Cáceres, José. "Declaratoria de independencia del pueblo dominicano." In *La independencia dominicana,* edited by Juan D. Balcácer and Manuel A. García, 213–19. Madrid: Editorial Mapfre, 1992.

Ojito, Mirta. "Immigrants' New Road Leads to Suburbia." *New York Times,* September 30, 1996, B1–2.

O'Neill, Hugh, and Mitchell L. Moss. *Reinventing New York: Competing in the Next Century's Global Economy.* New York: Urban Research Center, Robert F. Wagner Graduate School of Public Service/New York University, 1991.

Onis, Juan de. "Dominicans Crowd 3 Roads Leading out of Poverty." *New York Times*, May 15, 1970, A3.

Ortiz Puig, José Augusto. *Emigración de libertos norteamericanos a Puerto Plata en la primera mitad del siglo XIX: La Iglesia Metodista Wesleyana.* Santo Domingo: Alfa y Omega, 1978.

Pacini Hernández, Deborah. *Bachata: A Social History of a Dominican Popular Music.* Philadelphia: Temple University Press, 1995.

Pellegrini, Elena. "Locating Sites of Memory in Art of the Dominican Diaspora." In *Art in Transit: A Dominican Experience*, 23–29. New York: INTAR Latin American Gallery, 1996a.

———. "Artist Biographies." In *Modern and Contemporary Art of the Dominican Republic*, edited by Suzanne Stratton, 113–22. New York: Americas Society and the Spanish Institute, 1996b.

Pérez, Glauco. "The Legal and Illegal Dominicans in New York City." Paper presented at the Conference on Hispanic Migration to New York City: Global Trends and Neighborhood Change. The New York Research Program in Inter-American Affairs at New York University, December 4, 1981.

Pessar, Patricia R. "The Role of Households in International Migration: The Case of U.S.-Bound Migrants from the Dominican Republic." *International Migration Review* 16, no. 2 (1982): 342–62.

Phillips, Genaro. Remarks. In *Caribbean Visions: Contemporary Painting and Sculpture*, 124–25. Alexandria, Virginia: Art Services International, 1995.

Portes, Alejandro, and Luis E. Guarnizo. *Capitalistas del trópico: La inmigración en los Estados Unidos y el desarrollo de la pequeña empresa en la República Dominicana.* Santo Domingo: Facultad Latinoamericana de Ciencias Sociales/ Proyecto República Dominicana, 1991.

Portes, Alejandro, and Robert Bach. *Latin Journey: Cuban and Mexican Immigrants in the United States and Latin America.* Berkeley and Los Angeles: University of California Press, 1985.

Ramírez, Nelson. *"Los cambios en la planificación familiar y la fecundidad en República Dominicana: Relaciones e implicaciones."* Santo Domingo: Instituto de Población y Desarrollo, 1991.

———. *La emigración dominicana hacia el exterior.* Santo Domingo: Instituto de Estudios de Población y Desarrollo, 1993.

Riley de Dauhajre, Elizabeth. "Pobre consumidor dominicano." *El Listín Diario*, Sábado Económico. April 29, 1995: 1.

*Report of the Commission of Inquiry to Santo Domingo.* Commissioners B. F. Wade, A. D. White, and S. G. Howe. Washington, D.C.: U.S. Government Printing Office, 1871.

Reubens, Peggy. "Psychological Needs of the New Immigrants." *Migration Today* 8, no. 2 (1980): 8–14.

Roberts Hernández, Wilson. *Eduardo Brito: 1905–1946.* Santo Domingo: Biblioteca Taller, 1986.

Rodríguez Demorizi, Emilio. *Próceres de la Restauración: Noticias biográficas.* Academia Dominicana de la Historia. Vol. 12. Santo Domingo: Editora del Caribe, 1963.

————, ed. *Papeles de Buenaventura Báez.* Academia Dominicana de la Historia. Vol. 21. Santo Domingo: Editora Montalvo, 1969.

Roggiano, Alfredo A. *Pedro Henríquez Ureña en los Estados Unidos.* State University of Iowa Studies in Spanish Language and Literature. No. 12. México, D.F.: Iowa University, 1961.

Rohter, Larry. "Flood of Dominicans Lets Some Enter U.S. by Fraud." *New York Times,* February 19, 1997.

"Rubirosa, Porfirio." *Enciclopedia Dominicana.* 3d ed. Vol. 6, 157–60. Santo Domingo: Enciclopédica Dominicana, S.A., 1986.

Sainz, Rudy Anthony, "Dominican Ethnic Associations: Classification and Service Delivery Roles in Washington Heights." Ph.D. diss., Columbia University, 1990.

Santana, Isidoro, and Magdalena Rathe. *Reforma social: Una agenda para combatir la pobreza.* Santo Domingo: Editora Alfa y Omega, 1993.

Santana, Isidoro, and Antonio Tatis. "Tendencias recientes y perspectivas de la situación ocupacional en R.D." *Población y Desarrollo* 9 (1985): 1–35.

*Santo Domingo: A Paper from the Knickerbocker Magazine.* New York: American West India Company, 1863.

Sassen-Koob, Saskia. "Formal and Informal Associations: Dominicans and Colombians in New York." In *Caribbean Life in New York City: Sociocultural Dimensions,* edited by Constance R. Sutton and Elsa M. Chaney, 278–96. New York: Center for Migration Studies, 1987.

————. *The Mobility of Labor and Capital: A Study in International Investment and Labor Flow.* Cambridge, England: Cambridge University Press, 1988.

Schoenrich, Otto. *Santo Domingo: A Country with a Future.* New York: MacMillan Co., 1918.

Serrulle Ramia, José. *Economía y construcción.* Santo Domingo: Ediciones Gramil, 1984.

Sención, Viriato. *They Forged the Signature of God.* Trans. Asa Zats. Willimantic, CT: Curbstone Press, 1995.

Shea, Steven, et al. "The Washington Heights-Inwood Healthy Heart Program: A 6-year Report from a Disadvantaged Urban Setting." *American Journal of Public Health* 86, no. 2 (1996): 166–71.

Shorris, Earl. *Latinos: A Biography of the People.* New York: Avon Brooks, 1992.

Silfa, Nicolás. *Guerra, traición y exilio.* Barcelona: The author, 1980.

Sumner, Charles. "Naboth's Vineyard." In *Charles Sumner: His Complete Works.* Statesman Edition. Introduction by Hon. George Frisbie Hoar. 1900. Reprint. New York: Negro Universities Press, 1969.

Susann, Marian. "María Montez: On and Off Camera." *Latino Stuff Review* 15 (1994): 3–4.

Tactuk, Pablo, et al. "Estudios determinantes, niveles y tendencias de la fecundidad en la República Dominicana." *Población y Desarrollo* 1 (1991): 9–29.

Tansill, Charles Callan. *The United States and Santo Domingo: 1798–1873.* Baltimore: Johns Hopkins University Press, 1938.

Tejeda, Juan de Dios. "De Juan de Dios Tejeda a Ramona Ureña." *Familia Henríquez Ureña: Epistolario,* 281–83. Publicaciones del Sesquicentenario de la Independencia Nacional. Santo Domingo: Secretaría de Estado de Educación Bellas Artes y Cultos, 1994.

Thomas, Jr., Robert McG. "Ilka Tanya Payán, 53, an Actress, Dies; Champion for Anti-AIDS Causes." *New York Times,* April 8, 1996, Obituaries, B12.

Torres-Saillant, Silvio. "Dominicans as a New York Community." *Punto 7 Review: A Journal of Marginal Discourse* 2, no. 1 (1989): 7–25.

———. "La literatura dominicana en los Estados Unidos y la periferia del margen." *Punto y Coma* 3, nos. 1–2 (1991): 139–49. Reprint. *Brújula/Compass* 11 (1991): 16–17. Reprint. *Cuadernos de Poética* 7, no. 21 (1993): 7–26.

———. "The Dominican Republic." In *No Longer Invisible: Afro-Latin Americans Today,* edited by Minority Rights Group, London: Minority Rights Group, 1995.

Ugalde, Antonio, Frank Bean, and Gilbert Cárdenas. "International Return Migration: Findings from a National Survey." *International Migration Review* 13, no. 2 (1979): 235–54.

Unanue, Manuel de Dios. *El caso Galíndez: Los vascos en los servicios de inteligencia de EE. UU.* New York: Editorial Cupre, 1982.

Vega, Bernardo. *En la década perdida.* Santo Domingo: Fundación Cultural Dominicana, 1990.

———. *Trujillo y las fuerzas armadas norteamericanas.* Santo Domingo: Fundación Cultural Dominicana, 1992.

Vicens, Lucas. *Crisis económica 1978–1982.* Santo Domingo: Editora Alfa y Omega, 1982.

Vicioso, Sherezada (Chiqui). "Dominican Migration to the United States." *Migration Today* 20 (1976): 59–72.

Vincens de Morales, Margarita. "Síntesis biográfica de María Montez." *Isla Abierta.* Suplemento de *Hoy,* March 6, 1993: 3.

———. *María Montez: Su vida.* Santo Domingo: Vincens & Morales, 1994.

Waldinger, Roger. *Through the Eye of the Needle: Immigrants and Enterprises in New York's Garment Trade.* New York: New York University Press, 1986.

Watkins, G. A. "Childhood Vision Comes True for Young Dominican Assistant District Attorney." *Raices* 2, no. 2 (1997): 18–19, 22–25.

Welles, Sumner. *Naboth's Vineyard: The Dominican Republic, 1844–1924.* 1928. Reprint. 2 vols. Mamaroneck, N.Y.: Paul P. Appel, 1966.

Williams, Terry. *The Cocaine Kids: The Inside Story of a Teenage Ring.* Reading, Mass.: Addison-Wesley, 1989.

# Index

**About the Authors**

SILVIO TORRES-SAILLANT is Assistant Professor of English at Hostos Community College, CUNY, and the Director of the CUNY Dominican Studies Institute at The City College of New York. He is a native of the Dominican Republic and has lived in the United States since 1973. He is also author of *Caribbean Poetics* (1997).

RAMONA HERNÁNDEZ is Assistant Professor in the Latino Studies Program at the University of Massachusetts at Boston and a Research Associate in the CUNY Dominican Studies Institute. She was born in Santo Domingo, the Dominican Republic, and has lived in New York City since 1973. She is coauthor of *Dominican New Yorkers: A Socioeconomic Profile* (1995).